WHAT'S AHEAD *&* MEANWHILE

WHAT'S AHEAD & MEANWHILE

BY

EDWARD SANDFORD MARTIN

Essay Index Reprint Series

BOOKS FOR LIBRARIES PRESS
FREEPORT, NEW YORK

INTERNATIONAL STANDARD BOOK NUMBER:
0-8369-2325-1

LIBRARY OF CONGRESS CATALOG CARD NUMBER:
74-156688

PRINTED IN THE UNITED STATES OF AMERICA

CONTENTS

CONTENTS

WHAT'S AHEAD & MEANWHILE

Our Convalescent World

HERE IS NO USE IN OBJECTING BECAUSE people don't do what you think they should, especially in public concerns. The affairs of this world and this life are very incompletely transacted by people who do as you think they should. Most things that happen happen largely as a result of the activities of persons who do what you think they shouldn't or of the failure to function of persons on whom you had built hopes.

Take the War! It was pretty much all a consequence of mistakes—the great preliminary mistake, well-distributed, of starting it: von Kluck's mistakes that led up to the battle of the Marne, the mistakes of Gallipoli, and so on through four years of it until in spite or in consequence of all mistakes, the end came.

Take the Peace! Here we are, at this writing, in the earlier weeks of a political campaign, which aims chiefly to get the opinion of the country as to who made the worst mistakes after the War.

The great factor in history that is constant is the fallibility of man. The one thing we can count on in life is that people will blunder. One might just as well expect that in the first place and try to be reconciled to it. It is the way the world is run. Life is a hurdle race and mistakes are the

I

hurdles, and yet people groan about them and complain of them as though they didn't belong in the game. But of course they belong in it, and the winner is the contestant who best and soonest gets over them.

One of the most useful exercises is to attempt something you have never done and think you can't do. To do it you have to amend, enlarge, extend yourself, and if you do that it may be a bigger thing than to accomplish what you undertook. For to amend ourselves, enlarge and extend ourselves and become more than we began, is precisely what we are in this world for. We are started in life with the admonition to make the most of our talents. Education and all influences supposed to be beneficial are directed to induce us to let out a tuck and try to amount to something. But most of us hate to do it. We hate to think; we hate exertion; we hate discipline and self-denial; we hate innovation.

All these phenomena can be observed on a large scale in our present world. For practical purposes it is a newborn world, invited to amend itself and to undertake much more than it finds ability to do. It must recontrive its life, and it does not want to. It has come through a terrific struggle to be born again, and is still tired. It hates to think, it hates exertion and a large part of it hates innovation. Nothing can make it bestir itself sufficiently and submit itself to necessary changes, but the discomfort of things as they are and the fear of what they may be if they are not taken in hand. It is the old-fashioned fear of hell, prodding up a reluctant world to go after salvation. The whimperings and complaints of people who think life ought to go on again in the old way, and can if proper plans are furnished and competent hands guide it, and their efforts to supply such hands and plans, are amusing when they do not threaten dangerous misdirection and delay.

We have had action, no end. The world has passed the crisis of a terrific sickness and these are days of convalescence, but of a convalescence hardly less anxious than the illness it succeeds. It is a convalescence full of pains and distempers, threatened constantly with relapses, needing careful watching and nursing all the time if the patient is to be saved from loss of vital powers and from age-long invalidism. Certainly in such times people who can sit down and think, have need to do it.

For there are more world problems nowadays than can be settled even at the polls. Indeed, the most that will be done at the polls, or in conferences or councils, will be to record something thought out elsewhere by people sitting apart, watching events and taking such council as comes of solitude and meditation. We have had a great row and delay and disagreement about the details of a mechanism designed to give a broken world a chance to get well of its fractures and bruises. The delay has held back the organization of the remnants left by the War and is generally credited with having done immense harm. But,

after all, the delay is only more of the same disease that made the War. The War did not cure the
disease; it ran over into the making of the peace.
What made the War? Vanity and fear; love of
riches and love of power. What has delayed the
peacemakers? The same—vanity and fear; love
of riches and love of power. Those are the things
that must be cured if the world is to get well and
those are matters that can always be meditated in
solitude. The cure of them is not political nor
economic, though politics and economics have their
places in it. It is spiritual. It will come, if
it comes, when the leadership of the world—the
controlling leadership—can find the political road
humanity should travel, and when humanity is
ready to travel it.

But it may be debated whether political leadership will ever find that road. Humanity may find
it by mass instinct. The question as to whether
leaders lead the herd, or the herd crowds them
where they ought to go, is not altogether easy.
People of great sobriety and judgment say that
no leadership can control the world at this time;
that the great forces that are working in it will
work out whether they are opposed or not, breaking
bonds and bans, their courses shaped by driving
instincts behind them.

The mass feels, and produces thinkers, and
presently a man of action. When the mass has
produced a great leader, the thing is to get something valuable out of him while he is still good,

because leaders spoil so fast. They swim in terrible twisting currents of adulation, solicitation, abuse, and condemnation. They are all black to one side, all white to the other. When they would stop and think, they are driven on; when they see the course and would pursue it, they are thwarted. Fool friends practice to twist them away from their best conclusions by arguments of expediency. Fool enemies assail them with slanders. It is an awesome calling to be a world leader, and men do not seem to last long at it. World leaders especially have need to sit apart, from time to time, and rest and look on at the world in continuous performance.

What sort of eggs is she hatching out, our Mother Earth, so unfamiliar and disquieting in her present gestations? What will come of all these vast upheavals, this general upset? How long will the Bolshevists last, and when they go how will they go? They will not make the world communist, but they may do something to it that will be more interesting to future historians than comfortable for present earth dwellers. What Bolshevism aspires to do has very slight relation to what it may actually accomplish. It is a moving, destructive force and will get somewhere, though probably not where its artificers think to send it. It is an exceedingly ominous force, and powerful just now by its partial acquirement of organization. If there must be a collective effort to fight it back from Western Europe, the issue of that effort will leave Europe different from what it found her.

There is not a country in Europe, not a country in Asia, in which the present order rests on a firm basis. We think we know, if we know anything, that England will still be England twenty years from now; that France will still be France. And Germany will be Germany, though Austria, it would seem, may be a spot on the map where there once was a nation. British will still be British; French, French; Italians, Italian; Germans, German; but what sort of British will govern England and on what plan, and with what visible results we do not know, nor who will be on top in Italy or Germany or France. And as for all the newborn nations, no one can foresee how many of them will grow up, nor who will run a nursery for them.

Optimism nowadays is based chiefly on religion. It looks with confidence for better times, and a truer spirit in men. It sees a lot of good in the world, both spiritual and material; it sees knowledge ever increasing, and, though it recognizes the danger signals and sees how slowly response comes to them and what grave impediments delay it, it does not think a world so laboriously improved as this of ours is really going to pot. But even optimism, though it has faith in the future, hesitates about the present. It does not know how far it is to the turn in the road that leads in the direction of harmony and happiness, nor how the going will be until we reach it.

Ourselves and Other Nations

HE RECENT DISCUSSION AS TO WHICH OF two citizens will be President of the United States, has been unlike any that has preceded it. It has had to do mainly with our relations with other nations. For the moment we are not popular among the members of the great family of Europe. They suffered extremely from the War and looked to us to do very much more to bring them back to peace, shelter, and regular meals than we have so far been able to do. It would be funny to observe how ill they think of us and what curious faults they find in us, if only we were better satisfied that we were really blameless. But in truth we are not ourselves entirely pleased with our own performance since the War ended, and the main discussion in the late campaign was about whose fault it was and what could be done about it.

Everybody must have had enough of that, but it may not be unsuitable to notice that, whereas most of Europe has been speaking cross words about us for about a year, and we have been busy blaming and reproaching one another for the last nine months, there are still left in England witnesses who still think of us with affection and write hopefully of our qualities.

Professor Gilbert Murray, writing recently in the *Manchester Guardian* about the Pilgrim fathers and their great adventure, fell into a discussion of the English and the Americans—meaning us of the United States—and what they think of one another. He said some really remarkable things about the feeling of the English Liberals toward their brethren here. "An immense mass of liberal-minded Englishmen," he said, "insist on regarding the Americans as something a little more than human, abnormally cool and generous and efficient, like the hero of a cinema play. We expect them," he said, "to be better than they are, and it is wonderful how angry it makes them."

"An immense mass of liberal-minded Englishmen!" That means a good many. Then Doctor Murray thinks a great many Englishmen have this feeling he speaks of toward America! That is consoling just now, even though our good friends may be too indulgent. He went on in that article, talking about the War, and how, just as soon as the British had read their own White Paper and convinced themselves that their cause was good, they "expected America, like a knight-errant, to ride romantically into the ring and strike down the oppressor."

"Is there any other nation in the world," says Doctor Murray, "of which we should have formed such an absurd hope? We are always expecting of America more than ought to be expected of any normal agglomeration of human beings."

Now that's extraordinary, isn't it? How many of us have ever had an idea that anybody had such sentiments about us as Doctor Murray expresses?

Distance, of course, lends its enchantment to trans-atlantic visions, but Doctor Murray has actually been here, and, in spite of knowing better, he shares these feelings that he speaks of. What faith they must have in us, these English Liberals! One may say that it is a faith in faith; a faith in what is in us somewhere, somehow, of which we are barely conscious. Some of it may have come from the Pil-grims whom Doctor Murray talks about and that would mean that it was part of a leaven which leavened England as well as these States. Not the whole supply of Puritan yeast was shipped out of the country to the coast of Massachusetts. There was plenty left at home, and we may think, if we like, that it is a spiritual sympathy between the Puritan in England and the Puritan in the United States that is at the bottom of the feelings which Doctor Murray speaks of.

We are apt to think of the English as a whole. They are apt to think of the people of the United States as a whole. Of course the British Empire is a whole, and the American nation is another, but neither is a whole in the sense that all the people in it are of the same mind. The same line of division runs through both of them. In most matters there is not really a division of sentiment between the British and the Americans. The divi-sion is between people of different aims and under-standings and runs through both countries. Like elements in England and here fight elements op-posed to them but they are not clearly defined. The leadership is a good deal in sight; the followers not.

Average Americans don't know much about English Liberals. They don't know English politics. They don't know now what party is in power in England, or just what combination of parties. Doctor Murray speaks with the vehemence of disappointment of the "hideous outbreak of international blackguardism which dominated the general election of 1918," with results to the Treaty of Versailles that English Liberals lamented. That "queered the pitch," he says, "for any wise or generous reconstruction of Europe. It determined the downward road of European civilization and, in spite of occasional convulsive struggles from the British Prime Minister, handed over the main direction of policy in France and England to the worst elements in public life." We are used to having Mr. Wilson blamed for everything untoward that happened at the Peace Conference, but here is Doctor Murray, an English Liberal, offering Europe, England included, to share guilt with him!

What sort of an Englishman was it, what type of Englishman, that represented England in that "queering of the pitch," for any generous reconstruction of Europe? One may imagine it was the type of Englishman that goes through the world on the lookout for property and power for the British Empire; who wants anything that is good, who takes anything he can get, and hangs on like grim death to anything he takes. He is a valuable man, much respected in this world for the work he has done in it, but he excites apprehensions. A good example of him is described in two letters by John

Hay. They were written from Washington, where a commission of Englishmen, Canadians, and Americans had been sitting to try to settle questions in dispute about the boundary line between Canada and Alaska. Lord Herschell was the leading representative of Great Britain, and Mr. Fairbanks, afterward Vice President, was the leading man for us. Mr. Hay wrote to Henry White, Secretary of the Embassy in London, on December 3, 1898:

I hear from no less than three members of our Canadian commission that by far the worst member of the commission to deal with is Lord Herschell, who is more cantankerous than any of the Canadians, raises more petty points, and is harder than any of the Canadians to get along with. In fact, he is the principal obstacle to a favorable arrangement.

He wrote again to Mr. White a month later:

Lord Herschell, with great dexterity and ability, represents his own side as granting everything and getting nothing, and yet I think the letter of Fairbanks shows with perfect clearness and candor that we are making great concessions and getting no credit for them.

In the case of Alaska, it is hard to treat with patience the claim set up by Lord Herschell that virtually the whole coast belongs to England, leaving us only a few jutting promontories without communication with each other. Without going into the historical or legal argument, as a mere matter of common sense it is impossible that any nation should ever have conceded, or any other nation have accepted, the cession of such a ridiculous and preposterous boundary line. We are absolutely driven to the conclusion that Lord Herschell put forward a claim that he had no belief or confidence in, for the mere purpose of trading it off for something substantial. And yet, the slightest suggestion that his claim is unfounded throws him into a fury.

Lord Herschell was a very eminent and able lawyer, doing his best according to his lights for his client, and apparently not so appreciative as he might have been that a just settlement of a difficult controversy between the United States and Great Britain was more important than even the acquisition of harbors in Alaska. The upshot of it was that so long as Lord Herschell had charge of that matter no settlement could be reached, and the commission gave it up. It was settled afterward in London by men of a more accommodating disposition—Mr. Hay, Mr. Choate, Lord Salisbury, Lord Lansdowne, and a whole new commission—who were able to agree.

To understand Lord Herschell as Mr. Hay described him helps to an understanding of the kind of man that in international discussions makes trouble for the world. It helps to an understanding of the difficulties of the Peace Conference, for the spirit of Lord Herschell is not confined to English Tories, but it is to be found in all countries—here, in France, in Italy, everywhere—working unreasonably for material advantage, and bent on getting at any cost the most possible for its own. It is that blind spirit of national selfishness beyond the warrantable obligation to care for one's own that is the cause of wars and the great peril to the peace of nations. Happily it is no more characteristic of the mass of the British than of the mass of other peoples but it is strong, and when it gets the direction of a country's affairs it is infinitely troublesome and dangerous. It is often in power in Great

Britain, and, having the greatest machine in the world behind it, it has often made trouble. It is a spirit that understands force, but not much else, and that yields to prospect of force when nothing else can move it.

But there is another spirit in England—a great spirit, none nobler and saner, more just and wise, in all the world, that fights the English greed, and it is that spirit that ever reaches out toward its fellow in these States. After the Peace Conference had gone a good deal wrong, as English Liberals saw it "we only trusted more and more blindly," Doctor Murray says, "that America would come to the rescue of Liberal principles and international decency. We felt as if, obviously, so that every American could see, the people temporarily governing us were not England. The real England which hated militarism, which only wanted to help Central Europe, to appease Ireland, to rebuild Armenia, which never thought at all about oil wells and imperial tariffs, was more desperately in need of help than ever before in history, and it seemed obvious that America should see the need and bring the help."

He still thinks, this English Liberal, that the United States will somehow, somewhen, join the League of Nations and help to make it a real league and turn the tide of the world's fortune. Is it not extraordinary that such sentiments about us should exist in the mind of a well-informed person in any part of this world? And yet, when you come to think of it, corresponding sentiments do exist in the minds of well-informed people here. They would do all that Doctor Murray would have them do, not because they love England immoderately, not because they are infatuated with France, nor with Italy, nor with Ireland, nor with China, nor any other country; but because it looks right to them, and it is in them to do it if they can. They have sense enough to know that if they don't do, or try to do, what looks right to them, they will never get anywhere much, either in this world or the next.

People cannot live on other people's characters; at least, they cannot live a developing life so. Character may keep the world going, and character-less people may go on existing in it who would crumble and squash out if the organization was not kept up; but for purposes of development one must have some character himself and live on it and work it out.

We rejoiced to get into the War, not primarily to save our necks and our money, not to meet the peril to ourselves while we still had help, not altogether to save France or to save England, though those considerations touched our affections with a tremendous appeal, but, most of all, to save our own souls. The great determining motive for American action was spiritual. Many, even of the most ardent sympathizers with the Allies, doubted for a long time whether the quarrel was really ours. They knew where their hearts were, but they knew that the implication of a hundred million Americans in a European war, with all the sacrifices involved, should be based on nothing less than an irresistible summons of duty. We whose hearts said to us: "Get in! Get in!" despaired for long of getting a warrant sufficiently compelling to justify national action in a country which after all, was divided in sympathies. Action could not come until by the course of events it became a clear case accepted by the mass of our people of, "You'll be damned if you don't." We got into the War to save our own souls, to save ourselves from the appalling spiritual consequences of a vast duty put aside in a tremendous world crisis. We went in to save our own national existence, not because we feared the Germans would ever destroy us—for that fear was never prevalent in this country—but because we knew that a selfish country, deaf to its obligations to mankind, could never amount to anything worth being. We went in because we knew that our default in that crisis, if we did default, would have to be atoned for eventually by sorrow and disgrace, and belated repentances immeasurably more costly than prompt and timely action.

And so, in time, we shall get into the Peace and into the League in whatever form it finally takes, when the wit of man, and further experience, have done their best for it. What the world must learn before there can be lasting peace is that it is no gain to a country to take what does not belong to it. The division of territory has reached a point where that understanding is necessary. And yet there must go with it the further knowledge that civilization cannot be permanently held back by control of

important territory by people incompetent to keep
up with civilization. The parable of the talents is
true of nations. Progress is a law of life and the
nation that cannot, in time, develop what it has,
cannot hold its own.

What the Colleges Must Teach

APRIL 1921

NE HEARS THAT A LARGE PROPORTION OF the young men now in the colleges are restless and disinclined to stay through the course. Apparently they have a feeling that in the present state of human affairs what they can get in college may not be worth the time required to get it. That was true of the young men who went from the colleges to the War—when they got back again to college life it seemed tame and futile to them. Their younger brothers, it would seem, are feeling much as they did. From Oxford and Cambridge, England, a report comes that the undergraduates there are very much interested, but perhaps life outside the colleges in England is less solicitous just at present than the general life of our American world is, or, possibly, what is taught in them gives better satisfaction.

And yet there are reasons why the college boys may be restless. Possibly the English lads were so much more thoroughly worked out and tired out by the War that the university shades and the repose they foster are grateful to them. No doubt they feel the need of an interlude—of time to think things over and to think them out, before enlisting in the competitions of civil life.

Interludes in which to think are very useful, and there are people who think of the whole of college life as an interlude between school days and the conscious beginning of one's career. Ordinarily college boys take very kindly to that idea. One can understand that in times now past when human life was approximately constant, a fairly leisurely preparation for it was, for those who could afford it, a natural provision. The average boy who went to college went there in a tranquil spirit of adventure, to get what there was, or as much of it as he could, and to enjoy the getting of it. He accepted what was put on his plate, took it for granted that it was wholesome because the college had offered it, consumed it according to his ability, and in due time departed more or less cheerfully out into the world. It was assumed in those days that teachers and purveyors of education knew more about the larger life outside the colleges than undergraduates did. It was assumed that colleges knew what they were about, and that they were good to go through on the terms offered.

But now—oh my! Who can say that life is constant in these days, when one lives by the day and wonders what he and the rest of the world will be up against next? When every other newspaper tells the undergraduate that the world is not yet rearranged, that it is a new era, and no one knows what the conditions of life are going to be, is it surprising that he should ask himself whether the college purveyors are giving him real food that will help him to live, or are merely keeping him amused and employed by things that are out of date and no longer important? Educating a college boy nowadays is a good deal like building a battleship. In both cases the question comes up: Is this thing that we are putting money into going to be any good, or is some new final machine coming along that will sink it? It has been bad enough for the last fifty years, since educators began to lay off the old classical education and substitute for it something that seemed likely to be more useful in actual life, but at least in those years they had the advantage of knowing more or less what actual life was going to be, whereas now they have to guess at that, and then guess how to meet it.

If they are to guess right they must have more than mere knowledge of material means and processes. They must get a true conception of what human life is, and of what it is going to be—of what it must be if civilization is not to fall apart and go to grass for a long time preparatory to a new effort of humanity to get somewhere. If the colleges are to retain their importance they must be able to impart this spiritual leading to minds that are fit to receive it. If they don't, they fail in their most vital office, in the use that most of them were originally founded to serve. If they fail in that they lose their leadership, which will go to men of faith, as it always does. If they serve only secondary uses, albeit important ones, it becomes a question whether they are worth the money they are constantly asking for and acquiring, to keep them going on their present scale. If they cannot give true direction to fit minds, it may be as well that they should experience short commons and the *res angustæ* for a time, until their spiritual perceptions are quickened by a course of fasting and they get a new idea of the scope of their errand.

It was a curious fact that the presidents of nearly all the great universities lined up in the late election on the side that had the support of the money interests of the country, whereas, as a rule, the majority of the faculties took the other side. The presidents were concerned, apparently, for the financial maintenance of their institutions; the teaching bodies rejected the leadership of the side that was most concentrated on material prosperity, and backed the one in which, in spite of all drawbacks, they found some traces of a spiritual purpose. They put the job of saving the world above even the desirable work of ministering to the immediate business necessities of the United States.

The colleges with their immense costs of maintenance and constant need of new money to keep up their scale of living seem to be in danger of getting into the condition of rich people who have extended their establishments beyond what even abundant means can carry, and who have to think of money first. They seem to be suffering from the habit of *having*—the reliance on material things and concern about them that checks the impulses of the soul.

What the colleges need is what all the world needs, and that is religion. And what is religion? It is that which connects the visible with the invisible life. The colleges need it not merely in chapel and morning prayers, not merely in the

Y. M. C. A. and the pious societies; they need it as the world does, in everything that goes on. There is more to this life than meals and money and the domestic relations. Not even the reformation of women's clothes or the diminution of divorce will save the world. The religion of the United States for a good while past has been a sort of religion of savings banks, of thrift and foresight, and quantity production of all useful material things. Thrift is good; foresight is good; even quantity production is good and very necessary in this overpopulated world. Money is good, and wealth is good, but they are all goods of a secondary quality. The world may have all of them and go distraught. Germany did have all of them, but it lost religion. Its idea of life was incomplete.

It was written the other day on the tablet in a cemetery that contains the grave of an American who died in the War and who was buried with French comrades in France:

Here men gave their all of human joy and hope. May their supreme sacrifice inspire in men of other lands and times a complete devotion to public liberty, order, and peace.

That was well said, but it was not enough. They died for more than public liberty, and order and peace. They died in a blind faith that they were dying for something worth while, and they were, and it was more, a great deal, than mere improvements in this fleeting world and ever-perishing life.

The world will never settle down into a mechanism of public order. Life is bigger than that. It asks for more. It will always struggle out of every cage that human ingenuity will devise for it. It will be free. It will progress, and true religion is an immensely progressive factor. It breaks laws of men when they need breaking; it demolishes tradition when tradition is outworn, and always it searches for knowledge—for more knowledge of the purpose of the invisible God in this visible earth, and of the laws to which human life is geared, and what that life is all about, and what comes next. That is the kind of religion that sometime must run through the colleges. How they are to get it, Heaven knows, but they must have it or they are no good. Prob- ably it will come to them from the outside. As the world gets it, they will get it. They are criticized for being utilitarian. In that they are like the churches. They teach what they know and are will- ing to teach something better if somebody will tell them what it is. But what they teach for the most part is all right—the fault about it is that it looks like the whole of knowledge when it isn't. It is just like the fault that Albert Nock imputed to the Puritans when he said that they tried to put out their Puritan conception as the whole of life, whereas it was not the whole of life. The prohibi- tionists do the same thing. They have a kind of savings-bank religion at the bottom of their efforts. They try to save the world by the compulsory cor- rection of its habits. They do some good of minor importance, but the world will never be saved by the mere correction of its habits. It will be saved by activities which spring from inspirations that take men out of themselves and make them godlike.

When William James said the best thing the college could do was to teach its young men to know a good man when they saw him, he said what was true enough, but it must teach them what is god-like in men. There is a great deal, and there is some of it in all men, and what the colleges must do is to teach their students to know it when they see it. It is not the exclusive province of religious teachers to teach religion. It is the province of all teachers, and a teacher who cannot do it is by so much less qualified for his job. Agassiz got religion out of dissecting fishes, and passed it on to his pupils. Darwin got it out of earthworms and passed it on, and did good, though it raised hob with current theology. It is in all the sciences and all the arts, and at the heart of all literature that is worth its place on the shelf. It flows through all life and, unless it is felt and recognized, the learner and the investigator cannot get to the heart of what is going on. The world is a wreck not because it had not thrift enough, nor food enough, nor commodities enough, nor armies and navies and guns and poison gas enough, but because it lost religion and could not recognize and apply the eternal laws to which men and nations must con-form if they are to live in peace. To search out and apply these laws and send out men who can recognize and apply them, is the great job of the colleges, as it is of the churches, the job by doing which they can earn their keep.

Robert Briffault declared the other day in the *English Review* that the world is suffering to-day more profoundly, perhaps, than at any previous period in its history, and that the trouble with it is that the human world in all its aspects—political, social, ethical, spiritual, æsthetic—has been built upon fictitious conventions, once held sacred, held at the worst to be expedient and convenient, and that those conventions are to-day no longer believed. That, and no less, he says, is "the appalling gravity of the situation." He finds the very ground on which the world stood to be cracking and sagging beneath it.

Faith, he said, can move mountains, but the process is not reversible. The need of moving mountains, be it ever so great, cannot help one jot toward supplying faith. No manipulation of old formulas, no amount of professed belief, can serve as the motive power of human action. "Our religious tradition, our political tradition, our historical tradition, our social tradition, our ethical tradition, are no longer believed; and, being no longer believed, they can neither move mountains, nor can they move the smallest cogwheel of the world's machinery by so much as a hair's breadth."

Now that, more or less, is what the colleges are up against. There is faith in religion—the Christian religion—a great deal of it, though Briffault does not seem to recognize it, but of all other things he speaks of it is very much as he says. Faith in them is gone. They were what the world was run on up to 1914, and what happened in the next four years still seems to most people sufficient evidence that the world had been run on them long enough, and that it needs new ideas and new application of them if it is to continue.

What are the colleges going to offer as a substitute for this vanished faith in a large part of what they have been used to teach? How are they going to help the young men in their charge to have faith in something and to discover what it is they can have faith in, and to work out the application of that faith to human life in years now ahead? Of course, a great deal of what the colleges used to teach is still teachable. They can teach chemistry and botany and physics and mathematics and Latin and Greek and more or less even of history. They are all good—they all belong to knowledge and knowledge is a useful thing. The great trick is going to be to persuade the young gentlemen that these branches are still worth acquaintance—that they still qualify persons who know them more or less to be more useful in life and even, some of them, to make a better living. A man is not going to study very hard unless he thinks something important or lucrative is going to come of it. If his studies make him wise, that is important whether it is lucrative or not, though it is apt to be lucrative too, but unless they do make him wise they won't help him enough, and unless he thinks they are going to make him wise he will hardly bother with them. It comes back a great deal to what William James said, that the great thing a college education might do was to make you know a good man when you saw him. It is good men, remarkable men, wise and able men, who are needed in the reconstruction of human life. They are not the current, but they may be very helpful in directing the current. The great current of life is sure to get somewhere always, but it goes better and arrives more fortunately if it gets wise direction. Above all things the college boys must be helped to believe in something. Something must be shown to them that they can trust; something must feel strong under their feet when they stand up.

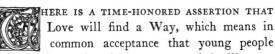

Living in the Country Again

MAY 1921

HERE IS A TIME-HONORED ASSERTION THAT Love will find a Way, which means in common acceptance that young people who develop a disposition to get married will somehow contrive to do it. Let us hope that this old saying is still valid, for it is highly important that young people who are so disposed should marry and continue the race. The main part of that work is up to them. There are edifying statistics to prove that the children of elderly people, and especially of elderly fathers, inherit a greater maturity of mind than others, and, on the whole, are more intelligent and wiser than the offspring of the young. The cases cited are impressive, but one recalls in defense of human nature the classification of untruths as "misinformation, lies, and statistics." However wise the elderly people's children are, there will never be enough of them to carry on human life, and the mass of the active population of the world will undoubtedly be contributed as heretofore by young parents.

The young will marry and somehow will live, even in these times, but how in the world they will manage just now, especially in the cities, and more particularly in this great city of New York, is matter for anxious thought for people concerned about their welfare. Housing costs so much. Food

27

is still so dear. Servants, if they have any, are so
expensive. The minimum income on which the
beginning of family life may be supported has come
to be a sum which must be formidable indeed to
young earners. The habit of society, or perhaps
we ought to call it the capitalistic system, is to pay
small salaries to beginners and reserve the big ones,
as a rule, to elders who have succeeded in competitions and got their hands more or less on the machinery of subsistence. Good young men, who have
been properly trained, can earn money from the time
they start in to do so, but they cannot always earn
very much, and unless there is someone ready to
help them out their case must be pretty difficult.

Nor can it be said that there is any immediate
prospect of its being much easier. One hopes that
things are progressing in the world; that the great
disturbance of life is settling down, that the unemployed will soon find work again, that the cost of
all necessaries will be lower; but still, this is a
world greatly impoverished by war, and it will not
get rich again, and living will not be cheap again,
overnight. The main part of the work of the world
now is done in cities. Some people live in cities because they like it. A great many people live in them
because they cannot make a living anywhere else.
People of moderate intelligence can keep alive in the
country with comparative ease, provided they are
reasonably robust and are willing to do a fair
amount of physical work, but to make a *good* living in the country requires unusual talent, energy
of mind and body, expert knowledge, and more or

less training. The mind must be adjusted to agricultural labor as well as the muscles. To live well in the country people must know how to be happy there. To keep alive they must have fun enough to keep them spiritually and mentally' healthy. They must have reading and companionship and reasonable pleasures. The main attraction about country life is not so much profits as the life, but life is not satisfactory unless the profits suffice for it.

Suburban life is a great solution for the problems of young married people, and in cities where suburbs are accessible and pleasant it is a good solution. Even in New York it is the best solution there is, and New York, with rivers on both sides of it, is not so much blessed with accessible and inviting suburbs as some others towns are. New York is so big that everything connected with it is crowded, and when the out-of-town tide sets toward it in the morning, and flows out again at night, all means and avenues of approach are overloaded. There are more people in New York already than can be handled comfortably, and the number is increasing all the time. Year after year enormous office buildings rise downtown and are filled up with office workers, who inundate the streets at noontime and are added to the crowd that must be moved night and morning in from their homes and out again.

What is going to cure this congestion in the cities? Most of it in this country has grown up in two generations. Sixty or seventy years ago people of the older American stock found repose for their souls in employment for whatever faculties they had, on farms and in thriving villages and in small cities. After the Civil War the towns began to drain the country and the country to fill up with imported inhabitants. That has been going on ever since and with increasing power all the time. But within twenty years a great deal has been done to make the country more habitable to the lively-minded. Telephone service has spread into it; rural delivery of mail has increased enormously, especially under the late administration; electric light and electric power have found their way far out into the rural districts; and Henry Ford has done a marvelous work by furnishing a cheap motor car, not too expensive for farmers, and such a marvel of rapid transportation as to popularize the reformation of the roads. Henry has looked upon this work of his (of course he did not do it all) and has seen that it was good, and shows signs now of wanting to help it still further by distributing in the country not only the product of his factories, but the factories themselves. He is not the only person who is working on that idea. Other great employers have come to realize that labor can be cheaper in the country than in town, because wholesome and pleasant life is easier provided there. Printers go to the country and start great presses in villages. There really seems to be the beginning of a movement to carry away from the cities as much as possible of the work that does not need to be done there.

Immense effort is made and pains taken to make
cities big. When cities grow, the land they are
built on increases in value, and the land they are
spreading toward also increases in value, and the
merchants who traffic in them get more trade and
the newspapers more circulation, so there is a
pecuniary motive for a lot of people to boost the
town, and they do boost it. They talk about it.
They advertise it. They glory in its being bigger
than some other city, as though size were the
thing of most consequence in all the world. Maybe
there is something in size. At times there is. When
you have got a big monster to beat, you need to be
fairly big yourself to do it. But size is of small
consequence compared with quality. Cities are big
and will be big because circumstances force a
growth upon them, or designing people induce
growth, but their size does not seem to be of much
importance, nor yet particularly delectable. Nothing
material is as important as most people think, and
everything spiritual is more important than most
people think. That cities should grow big is not
nearly so important as that young people of a
good quality should be able to marry and raise
families. People are the important thing—not the
number of them but the quality of them. In the
city where the more fastidious young people—not
the too fastidious, but those that are just fastidious
enough—do not dare to marry and go to house-
keeping, because they cannot afford it, the very
much less fastidious people do dare and do do it
by the thousand, and their children are the children

that get raised. People who can sleep three or four in a bed, and who do not care to wash very much, and whose nerves are well covered, can live and be happy where nicer people cannot.

The other day one of the newspapers quoted Matthew Arnold, mid-Victorian, as saying in an essay:

> Our coal, thousands of people were saying, is the real basis of our national greatness; if our coal runs short there is an end of the greatness of England. But what is greatness? . . . Greatness is a spiritual condition worthy to excite love, interest, and admiration; and the outward proof of possessing greatness is that we excite love, interest, and admiration. If England were to be swallowed up by the sea to-morrow, which of the two, a hundred years hence, would most excite the love, interest, and admiration of mankind—would most, therefore, show the evidences of having possessed greatness—the England of the last twenty years, or the England of Elizabeth, of a time of splendid spiritual effort, but when our coal, and our industrial operations depending on coal, were little developed?

All that is sound discourse. It is not the big cities, overcrowded and hard to live in, that make a country great, any more than it is coal. There are people in England who think and say that England will never again be so rich as she was—that she has passed the peak of her material prosperity and is going downhill, and they expect her to dwindle as a world power. They think her cities will fall into moderate decay and that the population will live mainly on the land and win subsistence from it as it used to. They quite like the idea. They think people under those conditions will be nicer, and more as they were in the time of Elizabeth that

Mr. Arnold speaks of. Something that would decay New York a little would really be a great help. Must we hope, as these Englishmen do, that the prosperity of our country and the growth of our cities will be abated enough, presently, as a consequence of war, for a larger proportion of fit people to be born?

Relief may come to us by poverty, but who will dare to trust to that? In spite of excellent chances of a collapse of civilization in eastern Europe, which would pull western Europe and England down to the lower levels of self-denial and teach the English how to be happy though poor, one hardly dare expect a sufficient abatement of prosperity in these states to solve our young family problems. We must think of something else. The problem is how to live on less or else how to have more to live on. The solution may work out at both ends. All reasonably well-to-do people can live on vastly less than they do. Food enough to support life, and shelter and clothes amply sufficient for health, are not too difficult of provision if the present machinery of the world is working right. The problem is not merely how to live a great deal cheaper, but how to live a great deal cheaper and still be happy.

Nobody minds short commons so very much in themselves. If everybody came down in the scale of living it would not be so bad. The thing that is trying is to have too many of the other people of one's own group have a great deal more than one has oneself. People do not very much mind reduced circumstances if the reduction is not extreme, but they do mind coming down in the social scale. They like what they are used to, and they like to maintain the relation to other people that they are used to maintain. Now the concern about other people and what they have and how they live can be diminished if there is strength of mind enough to control it. People, old or young, who have a sufficiently strong idea of life of their own, an idea detached from commodities, a spiritualized idea, can get along and keep their quality and live their life and grow in grace on something near to a mere provision of necessaries. If life is going to be spiritualized so that people will care very much less about material things, it will really make much less difference to them whether they are rich or poor, and that will help the young people to get married and raise families. They will do it if they have nothing worse to fear than a pinch and a struggle, but they may not do it if they see in it social decline. What we want is something that will help superior people who are valuable to life. But all kinds of people are linked together more or less, and material improvements that helped the superior people would doubtless help everybody, and the crowd would crowd just the same. That is one trouble about looking for extra-good results from the material improvement of the world, but some good results do come from it, because, just as superior people ought to bear want better than inferior people, so they ought to bear abundance better and put it to more profitable uses.

And surely the time seems to be coming when it is going to be more profitable to be intelligent than it ever has been. We seem to be on the brink of great discoveries. Discoveries and the applications of new knowledge have changed human life and enlarged its possibilities enormously in the last fifty years, but no one who knows much about such matters thinks that they have more than scratched the soil of possible knowledge. The more we discover and learn, the greater is our power to discover more, and of knowledge waiting to be discovered there is not merely no visible end, but no imaginable end. The more we know the more enlarged becomes our estimate of the store of knowledge that is still hidden from us. Since wireless telegraphy has been domesticated and harnessed, it is a hardy forecaster who can say what the next thing will be. There are secrets of cosmic energy and atomic energy the discovery of which may supply power so easily and cheaply that the coal and the oil that are left may stay in the ground, while the power hidden in electrons is suspected of being more than is safe to discover in the present state of moral infirmity. Even now a true co-operation of the people of the world would produce such an abundance of the means of supporting life that the population of the world would doubtless have a fabulous expansion. That is the trouble with that idea. Get a huge increase in the means of support and the population will rush to meet it and doubtless will swamp it in time. You cannot improve the world very much by feeding it with more riches to support more people.

You can help it to amount to anything only by raising the quality of the people in it, and you can do
that only by spiritual means.

Meanwhile, while we are waiting for these improvements in life, and thousands of thousands of
excellent young people are waiting to get married,
there is really quite a good prospect of a better
patronage of country life, and a back-set in the
migration to the cities. Perhaps the tide has really
begun to set the other way. For two generations
the country has poured into the towns. The towns
always have poured back more or less, but now the
back stream seems to be getting really stronger.
This very cost of life for young people that we are
talking about will tend to make it stronger. People
will live where they can. If it is too hard or too
unpleasant or too unhealthy to live in town, and if
they conclude that their children's nerves will be
worn out before they grow up, more and more of
them will manage somehow to tie up to the country,
and more and more of them will probably get used
to it and like it. If they have character enough they
can do it. If they have character enough they can
live almost anywhere, do almost anything, and get
married when they get ready.

Cousin James

JUNE 1921

HE WORLD IS STILL TOO MUCH WITH US. While the War was going on, but before we were in it, people hereabouts were distracted from their natural pursuits because of what was hanging over mankind. The writers could not write the kind of books they had written. The painters could not paint. Day after day there was calamity piling up on Europe, and even over here, where we were comparatively undisturbed and in those days inordinately prosperous, the ominous disquiet of the times penetrated to us and occupied our thoughts and tired us and kept us tired. Vacations did not rest us, because we never got free minds. It was really better after we got into the War and were at work on our own end of it. Then at least we found vent for the disturbance within us.

The world was too much with us then, and it is now. We do not settle down. The state of Europe is still a factor in most of what we do and most of what we want. Still restlessness pervades the Western Hemisphere as it does the Eastern one. To be sure, we go about our employments busily enough. We have to, for we have our livings to make. To be sure, we do not read of great battles in the paper every morning, and there is not a day-by-day toll of thousands of dead. The critical

37

anxieties of the War have abated, but still we cannot see what life is going to be, nor make our calculations to meet it. To the problems of war have succeeded the problems of peace, and they are very, very tangled and disquieting.

Some immediate duties have become plain because of changed conditions. After an unusually sharp attack of domestic politics we have elected a new President. These attacks are periodical and we shall not have another for nearly four years. Meanwhile we ought to back the new Executive we have chosen with our best hopes and endeavors and more or less irrespective of party. He is our sole means of governmental action and has the great advantage of having a congressional majority of his own party that is disposed to carry out his plans. We have learned to appreciate the importance of this last condition. For lack of it we are suffering and the world is suffering many things that possibly might have been averted, or at least alleviated, if our late President and the late Congress had been of the same mind. Europe, when it looks to Washington, sees there again a government that can act. So do all of us, and that is a pleasant change.

But we do not yet see what action to take, and that seems bad, for it is highly important to Europe and all the world, including ourselves, that we should emerge from cross purposes and hesitations, discover our duty, and get to work to do it. Europe is disposed to lean on us as heavily as it can. It wants to know what we are going to do, because we are so great a factor in contemporary life that what its own action must be depends very much on what our action is to be. If we are going to join the League of Nations, it wants to know it. If we decline that, but are willing to combine with the other countries on some different plan, or on a plan that bears a different name, it might adjust itself to that. If we are to stand off and do what we can for ourselves without committing ourselves to any new scheme of international co-operation, that, too, it is important that Europe should know so as to devise means as best it can to make its repairs and start again without us.

But at this writing, with the new administration just getting under way, we don't know what our government is going to do about anything of international concern, and we grope about it not because our government is withholding its policies from us, but apparently because it doesn't yet know itself and is groping just as we are. The delay, though inevitable, is embarrassing.

As we think about the state of the world and the dangers that at present encompass it, and the prospect that the destruction of its valuable contents, so effectively begun in the War, may go on a good deal farther, let us consider what there is in it that it is most necessary to preserve.

Is it the books? Everybody knows how scholars bemoan the destruction of the Alexandrian Library. Libraries are important, because in them all knowledge is recorded. But, after all, you might save all the libraries of importance and, while they might be interesting to the survivors of civilization and to

collectors to come, they are not the most important
thing to save. A few small collections of really important books would hold all the recorded knowledge
human life requires. A large part of what is in the
libraries is junk—interesting, to be sure, but not
very important.

Are the paintings, the great paintings, so important to be saved? Paintings and sculpture and
works of art—Heaven send they may not be destroyed! They are delightful; they are inspiring;
but in themselves they are not vital. Human life
can get along without them.

And so it is with most of the material apparatus
of the world. If the world is to go on as it is and
the people in it are to be maintained in the fashion
in which most of them are now living, there must
be a good deal of this material apparatus. There
must be places for them to sleep in, places for them
to live in, plumbing, railroads, means to raise their
food, means to distribute it, roads, motors, factories,
and all such things. They are essential—they seem
to be—to the distended populations of some countries like Germany and England, but very little of
the apparatus is vital to human life. An Arab can
live in a tent on dates and a little grain and goat's
milk, and get along and make progress in life, and
do very high thinking if he has it in him. Other
people can do the like if they have to. Sir Philip
Gibbs told the other day about the immense social
changes that have come to England as a consequence
of the War; how the people who had actually
fought the War had been pretty well cleaned out,

and a good many of the people who stayed at home
and worked had made all kinds of money. He also
told about the extreme severity of taxation and how
the old landed gentry had to sell out to the war
profiteers, and of some nobleman with a famous
name, who had sold his family pictures and the
accumulated treasures of generations in his country
house, and now has the old house left bare and
empty, and that is all.

It breaks the heart to read about things like that;
but, after all, nothing that he sold was really important compared with what he had left. He had
left, I presume, besides the empty house, his family.
That, if it was good stuff, is what is important.
The human stock in the world is important. A
high-class human being is the really important product of civilization. Material things, no matter how
great the store of them, nor how perfect, cannot
carry on the world. It is people—the people who
are left in it, the great people wherever you can find
them, of whatever race, of whatever color, the wise
people, the kind people, the people of character
and of brains—they are the important things to
save. If you can save them and save their control
of affairs, if they have it, human life will go on;
more books will be written, more pictures painted;
everything men have ever done in the world will be
done again and will be done better. The old junk
may be charming; it is worth saving, of course;
but it is not the vital thing. The vital things are
the human mind, the human soul, the human substance. Save that and send it along, and civiliza-

tion will go on to new exploits. Do not mourn too
much for the loss of things, however beautiful, however interesting by association. Things can always be reproduced if the spirit that originally produced them can be kept alive in the world.

YOU may say that the end of life is to die, and
no one will dispute it. But in what sense do you
use that word end—in the sense of mere termina-
tion, or in the sense of achievement? Think of it
as achievement, and then when you say the end of
life is to die you will have got something different.
Also, you will have got something that is true. The
end of life is to die a gainer from having lived, to
die dismissed from a completed task, to die prepared
by one's existence here for service and progress in
the next phase of activity.

My cousin James died the other day. It seemed
to me he died very handsomely indeed—a death that
was really an achievement after long and curious
preparation. He belonged to the old order, but it
was not the order that has just broken down. To
that he objected a great deal, albeit in many particulars it was quite kind to him. The order that
he loved was much older, and largely, I suppose,
imaginary, for one never knows how much of any
past period of time is true to one's conception of
it, or how much that would be highly objectionable
to twentieth-century expectations was mixed in with
what looks lovely to the retrospective eye. Cousin
James was very dutiful in his way, and scrupulous
in meeting the obligations of the order he lived in.

But he did not like it. He had only a limited confidence in democracy. He wanted the best people
to rule, and he did not think democracy was getting
them, nor see how it was ever going to sort them
out and give them the necessary power. He was not
sure of the destiny of the United States, though he
hoped for the best about it, and in his heart was a
true patriot.

He hated change. He did not care for money-
making and disapproved of people who did. He
never earned any money that I know of, and I do
not think he ever saved any. He was relieved from
inconvenient consequences of those neglects by becoming in middle life one of the heirs of an old man
who had been very shrewdly attentive to accumula-
tion. While it was not yet too late for him to go
about and see the world, Cousin James fell into a
very comfortable fortune and took his mother by
the hand, and fared forth across the seas to see
what was there, and especially to see England, the
old England with its cathedrals and villages and
churches.

He was not married—he never married. Most of
his life he lived with his mother, a lovely woman
to whom he was attached with all the strength of a
nature very tenacious in affection.

All that another man might have done. But
Cousin James had a peculiarity—his chief intellec-
tual interest in life was the Church. He came of a
line of Episcopal clergymen, and something ran in
his blood that no treatment could dislodge. He tried
treatments that would have answered for ordinary

cases. He flouted hygiene. He drank rather more
than he should as long as he could, and smoked
cigars most of his waking hours, but his congenital
interest in the Church never abated at all. He
read Church history by the shelfful and really knew
it. The thing that he hated worst of anything—
next to the worship of riches—was Protestantism.
He was always mad at Protestantism because it had
spoiled the old Catholic Church, which was the
thing that had possession of his heart. He considered that it was the Reformation that had led to
the schismatic churches—the Protestant and Roman
Catholic. He liked, in a way, the Roman Catholic
Church, but he considered that the Bishops of Rome
had usurped powers that did not belong to them,
and believed, I think, that the Church of England,
Protestant though it was, was truer heir of the old
Church than the Church of Rome was.

I knew Cousin James about fifty years and he
always had in him these sentiments and these preferences that I have tried to describe. He never
was exemplary according to the prevailing standards, never particularly acquisitive nor thrifty, nor
ever pleased with prohibition, but the basis of his
thoughts was always religion, this old church religion that he seemed to have been born to. His
main occupation in life was reading, but he liked
music and architecture and painting. He could
play old-fashioned whist and did play it. He was
interested in his family, very fond indeed of his
friends, self-depreciative and overappreciative of
others if he liked them, and quite caustic and

amusing in his remarks about the people who offended his prejudices. Indeed, he was delightfully amusing on most subjects. He had not much will power for action, but a great deal for inaction. His ideas and his sentiments, deeply founded and pondered, were very little affected by what happened to be going on. He disbelieved in a great deal that most other men valued and he believed a great deal that other men had let slip. When his mother died he adorned the chapel of a church he affected with an altar and an altar piece, very beautiful, in memory of her, with an inscription inciting the pious to pray for the repose of her soul. In view of the Protestant disapproval of prayers for the dead, that was almost scandalous when he did it, but I believe the disapproval has abated since then. When it came to his funeral there were prayers aplenty for his own repose—all the ministrations, it seemed, that the old Church had ever provided. When I saw him the other day lying in an oaken box, quiet and tranquil with a crucifix on his breast, still protesting against Protestantism, I felt here truly was a man of faith, a man who, stumbling along through long years and wandering a good deal, still had never lost the thread that guided him, and finally had achieved the death that awaits the faithful.

It has gradually been borne in on me that a large proportion of his ideas are true, and that the world, which seems now to have come about, is quite likely on its next tack to progress in his direction. Control of the world by the Church was tried in the Middle Ages, and turned out to be rather worse than other forms of political control. We shall not have that back. But we shall regain confidence in the facts of Christianity—the facts that filled Europe with cathedrals and abbeys—and learn anew the power that is behind those facts, and how to apply it to the concerns of this life.

And perhaps there will come church unity—that catholic unity that Cousin James reached back to—simply out of increasing realization by Christians that the beliefs they are agreed about furnish a working basis for life and are incomparably more important than the things about which they differ. It is possible and conceivable that disunion will fall away from the Church like the shuck from a ripened nut, and not only that, but that the community of truth in all the great religions now on earth may bring them all into much more harmonious and progressive relations. It is true of all of them—true, at least, of their principles—that what they are agreed about is at least important enough to modify their disagreements.

How Can Preaching Come Alive?

IN GOOD OLD GRUB STREET TIMES WHEN the disrepute of the literary calling was its protection, no respectable character went into it for a living. Those times are gone. Any day we may see Congress, that guardian of American industry, besought to do something for the protection of writers whose field of employment has been invaded by outsiders. It may still be disreputable to be a journalist, but at least it is not disreputable enough to keep people out of that vocation who think there is something in it that belongs to them. It is getting especially to be the refuge of dislocated statesmen and serviceable citizens who have graduated from public office. Since President Roosevelt adjourned from the White House to the editorial rooms of the *Outlook* the bars of journalism have been down to graduates from offices of state. Just as the saloon, and more recently the stage, have been the refuge of successful prize fighters who wished to turn to account the public admiration their labors had brought them, so now journalism is the refuge of statesmen. Mr. Taft writes editorials and correspondence articles for a syndicate. Colonel House does the like. Mr. Marshall, lately Vice President, contributes discourse to another syndicate, not to mention the crowd of witnesses who

47

are giving testimony in books or lectures or newspaper articles of their labors in the War and what
they think of the labors of others.

It is a pleasant calling to be a writer if one
can make it go, as the dislocated statesmen seem
to have discovered. All of them must have learned
how much of government is done by newspapers,
and to all of them it must have seemed a natural
step from official desk to writer's desk. Too great
a multiplication of distinguished syndicate writers
is hardly to be desired by journalists because syndicate writers, by the process of duplication, fill a
lot of space. Perhaps Congress will be asked to
do something, and there is something that Congress can do. It can pension the ex-Presidents.
They will not be so likely to write for the papers
if they do not need the money their labors bring
in. There is no objection to their being writers,
but they ought to be able to stick to the more
dignified lines of composition—to write books.

Better still if they would take to preaching, for
there is a real dearth of preachers. The world
never needed effective preaching more, and there
never was a time when so many important people
seemed to know it. One expounder after another,
impressed with the difficulties and the tangles that
the world is in, realizes that a different spirit in
man is necessary to release it from existing complications, and proclaims that the great world need
is religion.

President Harding declared only the other day
that what the world needs is more Christianity.

Ex-President Taft has come out quite strong for
Christianity, excepting the miracles. H. G. Wells
had it revealed to him, as may be remembered,
that religion has got to come across. Herbert
Croly, of the *New Republic*, has written in that
imperfectly sanctified journal to the same effect.
There is a crowd of important witnesses to the
world's need of religion—to the great urgency of
that need. Yet the zeal of young men for the
ministry seems very moderate—only one candidate
in this year's graduating class at Amherst College,
which used to be a hotbed of piety! Of course
the work does go on, but, considering how white
the world is for the harvest, the supply of laborers
seems scant.

President Butler of Columbia College, in his
annual report last fall discussed the state of the
world and found it "significant that in this period
of vigorous, able-bodied reaction the world should
be without a poet, without a philosopher, and without a notable religious leader." He found "the
great voices of the spirit all stilled, while the mad
passion for gain and for power endeavors to gratify
itself through the odd device of destroying what has
already been gained and accomplished." There can
be no cure, he said, for the world's ills and no
abatement of the world's discontent until faith and
the rule of everlasting principle are again restored
and made supreme in the life of men and of nations.

Doctor Butler merely expressed vigorously and
well the sentiments which thousands of people

share. The case is not obscure at all. The ministry are quite aware of it. A great many of them are working overtime and are far from satisfied with the results of their exertions. The active minds among the preachers are quite alive to the great current need and are willing to do anything that is suggested and looks hopeful, and do do it with zeal; and yet somehow the Church is not yet getting results commensurate with its efforts and desires, or with the need of the times. The state of the world, though it seems to be slowly improving, is still full of perils, and liable to relapse. If the trouble was with the Christian religion—if that was defective or out of date—that would be one thing; but that seems not to be the trouble. The difficulty is to get it home to men; to make it live and do the work that it was designed to do.

PERHAPS the preaching is not yet good enough. Indeed, we can leave off the "perhaps" and make a flat assertion that it is not yet good enough. We need somebody that can preach like St. Paul, as Alexander Harvey lately described his preaching in the *Freeman*. Mr. Harvey apparently had been examining it, and he made out that St. Paul had an immense sense of news, and that he had one great piece of news that he was always putting out, and the diffusion of which he seemed to regard as his great and special mission.

Mr. Harvey sees him, and sees him very big, in his relation to this piece of news, "the most tremendous since the fall of Adam," which, Mr. Harvey considers, the other apostles were neglecting. "Paul," he says, "is never a mere press agent, instructed to make propaganda look like news, but a grown man with a big story, hampered by incompetent subordinates, hounded by censors, hiding from the police . . . yet always getting his copy in and lifting his circulation to heights that obliterated rivalry."

And what was this story, this "big story," that St. Paul struggled unceasingly to get out? What was his great news? Mr. Harvey always puts it in italics: *"Jesus Christ of Nazareth has risen from the dead."* That was his news—the resurrection of Christ; and Mr. Harvey considers that St. Paul, without newspapers, without any of the appliances of advertising, without the printing press, did get his great news around in a truly wonderful manner and by so doing established Christianity.

Perhaps that is the kind of preaching we need now, and it may be, and many think it is, that St. Paul's great message is precisely the one that needs diffusion at this time.

St. Paul was not a minister of modern training at all. He came to the task of preaching because he had a message. He never went through a theological school. He had to make his own theology, and there has been a good deal of fault found with the way he did it, but it is true, as Mr. Harvey says, that he did have a story and considered it a great story, and felt that, unless it was true, nothing much mattered. His writings are great

writings, marvelous writings; but it was not because he was proficient in rhetoric or composition.
It was because of something inside of him that
would come through. His writings got their form
and fire and music and penetration from the message that they carried. When that happens we
call it inspiration.

Mr. John Palmer Gavit lately quoted in the
Literary Review of the New York *Evening Post*
something that appeared thirty-one years ago in
the *Sun* about writing—to wit:

> You don't find feelings in written words unless there were
> feelings in the man who used them. . . . It is like the
> faculty of getting the quality of interest into pictures. If
> the quality exists in the artist's mind he is likely to find
> means to get it into his pictures, but if it isn't in the man
> no technical skill will supply it. . . . It isn't the way the
> words are strung together that makes Lincoln's Gettysburg
> speech immortal, but the feelings that were in the man.
> But how do such little, plain words manage to keep their
> grip on such feelings? That is the miracle.

That is the idea. It is the feeling in the man that
makes great writing and the same thing that makes
great preaching, and the trouble with the preaching nowadays must be that the preachers have not
the necessary feelings; that the right facts have
not possession of them. Is the world going to
pieces because the preachers do not preach what
they ought to, and is the reason why they do not
preach what they ought to that they do not realize
what is important? The thing that is important
is what Mr. Harvey calls St. Paul's great piece
of news, but how is that going to help the world?

A contemporary authority has said: "The minute
a man becomes absolutely convinced of eternal life
and gets the adjustment of his point of view that
enables him to see that life on earth is a preparation
for that eternity, all his values change and fall
each into its own place." St. Paul's great message
is the chief historical basis of the accepted relations of this visible world with the world invisible.
The task is to make people realize that certain
things like immortality are not theories of this or
that religion, but facts; living, operating facts,
which all religions must accept and realize and
put forward and live by if they are to get anywhere.

There is now a great activity constantly at work
and constantly spreading, the main end and object
of which is to make mankind accept St. Paul's
great news item with all its consequences, and
to believe, to feel actively, that the dead live, and
that life on earth is a preparation for more and
more important life to follow. It is true that the
minute a man becomes absolutely convinced of
that, all his values change and fall each into its
own place. The concerns of this world will still
be important to him because his work is still here,
but not so destructively important. They will not
be primary; they will be secondary, as they ought
to be. They will bear a relation to the things of
the next stage of life. Preaching that will bring
them to that relation is what is needed, but the
preaching we get is timid on that subject. It
shows something not so much like eagerness to

have immortality proved as an apprehension that
it may be proved in some irregular way. It will
hardly be proved with vividness enough to help
the world in its present crisis except in an irregular way. St. Paul's great piece of news seems
to need contemporary corroboration. It is so familiar that it has lost a good deal of its news value.
It is accepted by those who do accept it as something that happened a long time ago and has not
happened since. That is true enough. It has not
happened since so far as anybody knows, but a
great deal has happened since to verify it and
renew its force. Things that seem to make for
verification of it are now happening constantly,
but most of the preachers are afraid of them and
most of those who sit under the preaching do not,
perhaps, know enough about them to have any
opinion of their value. If there is great news
available for the preachers, it must be let out if it
is to do any good, and to let it out—to back it,
diffuse it, and put it over as St. Paul put over his
great news—is a mighty scary task, that all prudent people are going to avoid as long as they can.

Happily, St. Paul was not a prudent man. He
had a great conviction and all the courage of it.
His story was, of course, ridiculous to all the com-
mon-sensible people of his time. There was no
precedent for it; nothing like it had ever happened. Anybody who put out a story like that
ought to have a committee of his person, of course.
Of this great news that St. Paul had, Mr. Harvey
says, "There were a few poor Jews who were in

a position to corroborate the story, but the better
class of Jews deemed the whole thing a fake,
pure and simple." It was the same, naturally,
with the better class of Gentiles. Compared with
the story of the resurrection of Christ, the news
of modern spiritism, that the dead can speak
to us, has wonderful support. Some of the best-
known and most authoritative minds in the last
and the present generations have credited it and
affirmed the possibility of its truth.

Myers said, in his book on the Survival of Personality, that, in his opinion, except for psychical
research and its fruits, there would have been few
persons left in the world a century hence who
would have believed in the resurrection of Christ,
but as things are, or as they were when Myers
wrote, he believed that there would be few people
who did not believe it.

William James, who was not at all convinced
of the facts of the Christian religion, saw, nevertheless, a possibility of new knowledge that might
clarify and re-establish it. "I confess," he said,
in a letter written in 1884 to Thomas Davidson,
"I rather despair of any popular religion of a
philosophic character, and I sometimes find myself
wondering whether there can be any popular religion raised on the ruins of the old Christianity
without the presence of that element which in the
past has presided over the origin of all religions—
namely, a belief in new physical facts and possibilities. Abstract considerations about the soul and
the reality of a moral order will not do in a year

what the glimpse into a world of new phenomenal possibilities enveloping those of the present life, afforded by an extension of our insight into the order of nature, would do in an instant. Are the much-despised 'Spiritualism' and the 'Society for Psychical Research' to be the chosen instruments for a new era of faith? It would surely be strange if they were; but if they are not, I see no other agency that can do the work."

If there is news for the preachers that will make their message burn and live they ought to get it. St. Paul got his news at first hand—it was revealed to him so that he felt its truth with passionate conviction. It is impossible that the preachers or anyone else should preach the spiritual news of our day until they get it. When they do get it, they will preach it. The most that one can advise them is to look for it, remembering that it is not more incredible than what they undertake to preach, and that it corroborates that gospel and does not conflict with it.

Clergymen are individuals and not a group that thinks all alike. They believe and they preach each man according to the light that he can get, and if now there is, as Conan Doyle says, "a new revelation" constantly coming through, they will in due time get hold of that.

Faith or Unfaith

OCTOBER 1921

HE LIFE OF DISCUSSION IS RESPONSE. IF there is going to be good talk, somebody must talk back. There has been a good deal of response to a recent discourse of the present writer, and most of it brings approval, but one letter has come in that is so strong in objection and so specific in its reprobation that it really helps discussion. Here it is, nearly all of it, for readers to consider:

"I beg your pardon, but I can't tell you how sad your article in the July *Harper's* has made me feel. It has filled me with a sense of hopelessness. What's the use of civilization if, as we just begin to get away from the credulity and superstition of the dark ages, we are to turn back to them for the answer of the problems they are making in civilization that has been promising so much? It is *faith and religion*, the superstitious and futile hopes growing out of them, that have brought all our troubles upon us.

"Why deplore the lack of faith when we have the Roman Church, still potent and growing in the world? What has it done for civilization? Never has there been a nation or individual that fell under its spell that did not degenerate. The Protestant Churches are very little better. They serve mainly at present as a powerful influence which the wealthy use to keep in subjection the poor and simple-minded. There is not a preacher in the world to-day that is not practically the tool, slave, voice, of some wealthy man or group of men. During the last ten years I have been in almost every town in six Southwestern states and incog. have studied preachers and churches first hand. And what I have said is putting the truth mildly. I believe religion and the churches are the greatest drag to the progress of human development. Faith and religion never solved any problem. Facts and reason alone can answer. St. Paul said Christ was risen. But of what significance was that? His getting into the world and out didn't matter. His message alone counted. And the churches explain away all of it that doesn't fit their man-made dogmas or is unpleasant to the influential members upon whom their salary and success depend. A man to succeed in the ministry had better have the influence and good will of one wealthy man than a dozen Gods.

"The Bible is a wonderful book; but more wonderful for the untruth it contains. It doesn't make good; it can't make good because it is not facts or truth. No one takes it seriously, not even the preachers. Who turns the other cheek, who gives a cloak to the man who has stolen a coat, who loves his enemy, who returns good for evil? To be a Christian in the sense of living Christ's teachings is to be a mollycoddle. It's an ideal to preach, but foolishness to live. And to a really thoughtful person the Sermon on the Mount is not a wholesome

ideal, because its teaching contradicts the best in
human nature; more, it is inconsistent with itself,
for God does not practice toward his subjects what
he preaches for them to observe.

"No, by sticking to facts and sane reason man
will solve his problems, not in crazy unproved
vaporings of a Lodge or Doyle, who turn their
vaporings into good hard cash.

"One had as well talk of an immortal digestion
as an immortal soul—both are simply functions
of a physical organ. When the organ is dead the
function can't function.

"For ten years I have been on my back, fighting
for my life. I have made life, religion, soul (?),
etc., a study. *I know*, as ignorant and superstitious people will say when you ask them for
some proof of their faith. I know, is not a proof.
It is simply an admission of ignorance. One doesn't
have to say two and two make four because I know.
They can prove it. There is no proof that I am
not right. I have but a short time to live; the
thing that makes me most sad in leaving the world
is to see the tendency in the so-called educated to
go backward."

The writer of the letter is, or was, a clergyman.
He seems not to contemplate with much gayety of
spirit either the prospects of human life while it
lasts here, or the complete extinction that he thinks
will follow it. Why should he be made sad by an
article that takes the opposite view—that suggests
that religion is the hope of the world—that the

Christian religion is sound and true and is likely
to be revitalized by a new confidence in a future
life that is already spreading among men? The
only reason is that misery loves company, and
we are comforted by agreement even with our melancholy moods.

The letter of the remonstrating correspondent
is not true, but doubtless there is some truth in it.
The churches are faulty enough without doubt and
are a great problem, but they always have been
faulty. The ministers always have been faulty.
Doctor Hutton, of Scotland, said at Northfield the
other day of the disciples of Christ who came to
be Apostles:

> They were not great men intellectually nor spiritually, and
> are never mentioned by the Master except for reproof. Many
> had asked why they were selected. By any system of judg-
> ment known to man they were unfitted for their task.

That is probably true of most of them. They
were not great men except as their faith and their
message made them great. The same is doubtless
true of the mass of the clergymen to-day in all
communions. There are exceptional men, but it
does not appear that the mass of them are any
better in quality than the Apostles were when they
began. If they become great it will be due to the
faith that is in them and the message that they
carry.

But our remonstrant charges that ministers nowadays cannot give their message—that they are
subject to control of business men who run the

churches and object to preaching that is bad for
business. There is truth in that, but not so much
as he thinks. Mr. Eastman, a Presbyterian clergyman, who is concerned with the home missions
of that church and has been writing about its un-
finished business, found that the great obstacle to
the union of struggling churches in rural communi-
ties was that

one man "ran the church," as the people themselves expressed
it. He controlled the elders or the governing board, and if by
chance they ever got a minister who was too big a man to be
bossed, the church got rid of him as soon as possible—found
him "undesirable" or "unworthy."

That agrees with what we know of human nature. Churches have to be run and supported by
people who will do it, and those people usually
like to have some say about the teaching that
shall come out of them. It is the same way in
everything—the men that manage colleges, finding
the money that keeps them going, are apt to want
to know what is being taught, and, if the teaching
seems to them bad for business, they are apt not
to like it. It is the same thing in journalism. The
men whose business it is to supply the money are
concerned about the doctrine, and if the doctrine
interferes with their getting the money and makes
trouble for them, they want to suppress it. That
is how organization seems to be the enemy of truth.
Organization is powerful and has a large appetite,
and it must be fed. It involves more or less sub-
mission of individual opinion to the apparent welfare of the organization. When the opinions

suppressed are matters of importance and deep conviction, of course that makes trouble. Organization, and a lot of it, seems indispensable to modern life. Without it you cannot have good roads, nor good farming, nor enough good housing, nor enough transportation, nor great cities, nor great newspapers, nor Ford cars, nor most of the things that we think we cannot get along without; but organization is not indispensable to truth. On the contrary, the boot is on the other leg—truth in the long run is indispensable to organization. An organization that does not square with what is true will perish in the end. A church whose organization suppresses truth will perish as a church. A university that misses truth, or sells it out and runs after business and financial support, will perish as a university. There must be truth. Whether things square with existing interests or not, they must in the long run square with truth, or down they come.

Let our complainant console himself, if he can, with these reflections. Truth is mighty and will prevail. It will prevail, if necessary, over the ruin of everything else that exists. If he is right, and faith and religion are the great obstacles to human progress, down they will go. If he is right and the soul is only as immortal as the digestion, it is a hard case for souls, but truth will prevail. If he is right and the Sermon on the Mount is unwholesome and will not work, the Sermon on the Mount will go by the board and surely truth will prevail. If he is right that rich men run the

churches, so much the worse for them. There are
all sorts of rich men—some of them are quite as
wise as other people. As a group they are hardly
to be trusted with the discernment of all the truth
there is in religion. But neither are the ministers.
It is just as easy to imagine a minister preaching
what he shouldn't as to imagine him inhibited by
the control of business interests from preaching
what he should.

And one recourse the ministers always have
against all the church bosses: they can live the life
they profess to preach. If they do that—if the
spirit by which they profess to be guided—the
spirit of Truth and of Love—shines out of them
in their daily walk and conversation, they are un-
beatable. They will win even their bosses; for
church bosses, not invariably, but as a rule, are
not in the business of running churches to deceive
and control the simple, as our remonstrant says,
but because in their way they believe in religion
and want it, and if they see it in a minister they
will not let him go so easily as one might think.
Life is more than words, and words indeed are
little worth unless they come from some one who
lives them.

As a matter of fact there is ground for belief
that the Sermon on the Mount never seemed so
reasonable to so many people—never went quite
so strong in affairs of the world since it was
preached—as it is going at this moment. In the
immense muddle of the nations which the War
has left, the salvaging of the remnants of the world

seems more and more to depend on the willingness of men to forgive their enemies and indeed to love them.

Russia has been, or at least has harbored, the enemy of mankind. We have to turn about and feed her. Germany has tried to steal a coat and the thoughtful people, especially the financiers, are looking about to find a cloak for her. France and England and most of the other Allies want reparations from Germany and are racking their brains not only to know how they can get them, but how they can receive them without being ruined. The problem is so difficult that they may have to forgive her out of pure self-interest. There never was a time when so many people had begun to realize that behind the Sermon on the Mount was by far the greatest mind, the most astute, the most merciful, and the most practical, that ever came to Earth. Do even individual men hate their enemies? Plenty do, of course, but anyone who is grounded in even the rudiments of wisdom knows that it is a sorrowful and stupid business which embitters life; that hate is a kind of poison which no wise man will permit to exist in him if he can possibly help it.

And then, there is the matter of immortality about which our complainant is so discouraged. How about that? Is belief in it diminishing, or the contrary? Doctor Osler discussed it in 1904 when he gave the Ingersoll lecture at Harvard on Science and Immortality. At that time he said that personal indifference about it was the prevail-

ing attitude of minds—that we were Laodiceans—
neither hot nor cold—that the average man had
only two giant passions—to get and to beget—
and that these satisfied him. He looked neither
before nor after, but went about his business until
evening without thought of whence or whither.

"And the eventide of life," he said, "is not always hopeful; on the contrary, the older we grow,
the less fixed, very often, is the belief in a future
life. As Howells tells us of Lowell, 'His hold
upon a belief in a life after death weakened with
his years.' Like Oliver Wendell Holmes, 'We
may love the mystical and talk much of the shad-
ows, but when it comes to going out among them
and laying hold of them with the hand of faith,
we are not of the excursion.'

"If among individuals we find little but indifference to this great question, what shall we say
to the national and public sentiment? Immortality, and all that it may mean, is a dead issue in
the great movements of the world. In the social
and political forces what account is taken by practical men of any eternal significance in life? Does
it ever enter into the consideration of those controlling the destinies of their fellow creatures that
this life is only a preparation for another? To
raise the question is to raise a smile. I am not
talking of our professions, but of the everyday
condition which only serves to emphasize the contrast between the precepts of the gospel and the
practice of the street. Without a peradventure it
may be said that a living faith in a future exist-

ence has not the slightest influence in the settlement of the grave social and national problems which confront the race to-day."

So it was less than twenty years ago—ten years before the War. Let our complainant think what he may about it, but how does it strike the readers of these remarks? Is there more or less concern for immortality in 1921 than there was in 1904? Is the great mass of thoughtful and active people still so indifferent about it? Is immortality and all that it may mean still not an issue in the great movements of the world?

I think not—not by a very great deal; but that in so far as there has been change—and there has been great change—it has been in the direction of a great increase of interest in immortality and a great increase of confidence in it, and that nowadays, among those controlling the destinies of their fellow creatures, there are many who consider that this life is only a preparation for another, and among them are men at the very top of affairs and in the guidance of whose illuminated minds is the best political hope of the day.

After all, something did come out of the War besides destruction.

The Armament Conference

WO GREAT PROCEEDINGS FALL IN THIS month of December. One is Christmas and the other is the conference at Washington for the limitation of armament and the solution of other world problems. The thing to do, if possible, is to mix these two proceedings, for until the conference, or some succeeding one, makes a satisfactory performance, Christmas is likely to be a waning festival, and unless there is an infusion of Christmas into the work of the conference, the results are not likely to meet the situation.

The motto—the slogan, as one might call it—of Christmas and of the conference is precisely the same. For both of them it is "Peace on earth, good will to men," and that for once is pretty generally recognized, for in these days all pious texts look more practical than they did. Since the War they have taken on that new aspect. We all know that we need peace on earth and we all know and are constantly reminded—particularly on the quarter day when some of us have to pay a tax—how much we need it. We also know, or begin to realize, that we won't get it except at the price of good will to men.

Nothing narrower than that sentiment may guide the debates and decisions of the conference if they are to do much good. The Peace Congress at

Versailles got so far away from that ideal and
became so bedeviled with the fears and selfish aims
of individual nations that it did not bring peace
to earth in the degree that was hoped for. The
aim of this present conference—well understood,
even though not expressed—is to accomplish what
failed to be accomplished at Versailles. They
tell us that it will be a long conference, lasting
perhaps six months. If it develops a wise spirit and
shows ability to accomplish important things, the
world will practically be put into its hands for
medication. If it can work out the limitation of
armament and can reply successfully to the question, Who's who in the Pacific? there is no telling
how many other important points will be referred
to it.

The President showed how important he thought
it when he called upon everybody to pray for two
minutes at the hour when the Council assembled.
That recalls war times, when every day at noon
a gong sounded in the government departments in
Washington to call the war workers to two minutes of silent prayer. We were in earnest then
and the government was not too proud to use all
possible facilities. We had better use them all
again, for this conference is a very grave matter.
It is not putting it too strong to say that the world
looks to it and to us for salvation. It is constantly
put up to us that we are an indispensable part of
the machinery of the modern world, and that unless we recognize our importance and our duties,
and function as we ought to, there is no assurance

that civilization can recover from its recent set-
back. Not that it will die; it can hardly perish;
but it can be put back a long time, and if civilization is so put back, make sure that we shall be
put back with it. We shall not forge ahead on
our own account after failing in our duty to the
rest of mankind. National progress does not come
out of duty slighted, but out of duty met and ful-
filled. We cannot skulk, we cannot shirk, and hope
to get anywhere. Skulking and shirking are not
even good for business.

We have disappointed all the world by staying
out of the League of Nations. The sentiment is
only too general that without the United States
the League is too much like a bobtailed flush. So
long as entrance into the League looked like
duty to the American people, the great majority
of them wanted and expected to go in. Practically
everyone was for the idea of the League. Out of
a long, tiresome, political squabble came a state of
mind in these States when the purpose of the
League was lost to the recollection of many people,
and the defects of the Treaty loomed up big, and
weariness of the whole subject brought the country
to a dull acquiescence in any result. But the result that actually came was no result at all; it was
merely a postponement. It was not accomplishment, it was not a step forward; it was failure.
We had seen our duty and we had not been allowed
to do it. Out of the requirements of the Constitution and the misgivings or perversity of some
minds in Washington, we had been trapped into

dereliction. In the conference hopeful people see another chance for us—a chance to get back where we belong; to do, not so much what other countries expect of us as what we have expected of ourselves. The conference is our hope. It is for us to get behind it; to insist that it shall not fail; so to place ourselves that if it falls, it shall fall on us.

WE CAN do a great deal from the outside. The atmosphere the conference works in is very important. If we can create an atmosphere that will sustain its hope and encourage its best thoughts and best efforts, that will be a great service. It has a better chance than the Congress at Versailles because the War is far away and the consequences of it are better understood, and the immediate future can be much better calculated. There are sober second thoughts at the end of 1921 that were not available in the early months of 1919. At Paris, in spite of everything, much was accomplished, and an arrangement was contrived under which Europe was to go on and has gone on. If we had gone on with it, it would doubtless have worked better, but if any good has come out of our detachment from it, it is that by holding off we have delayed the medication of the world until its case was better understood and the doctors more competent to handle it.

But are the doctors now more competent than they were at Versailles? Has any great new mind come forward that seems to understand the case any better? Perhaps General Smuts might be so regarded. His influence has grown, but it was very considerable two years ago; but apart from him there is no new doctor, and Mr. Wilson, whose gifts were very highly regarded by very many people, has been laid off. We had better not look for any glorious results of that conference from the development of individual talent, for the talent is not in sight. We may more reasonably hope that the conference may prove to be the instrument through which the aspirations of the forward-looking people of the world may take form and go on.

All the forward-looking people should work together then to help that conference, and especially the religious people. Everybody should get over the idea that religion is something apart from knowledge and not practical. Religion is not a thing apart. All knowledge belongs to it, and it belongs to knowledge, and is a supremely important branch of it. Scientists have fallen too much into the way of thinking of it as an eccentricity of the human mind that is outside the precincts of science. Nonsense! Science is not so sacrosanct as all that. It is nothing but knowledge in the making—the sum of what scholars and students think is true at a given time. Its facts are unstable and its conclusions constantly change as knowledge increases, but it has a good name and is respected because, though often stupid, it is usually honest, and seeks truth. The facts of religion—of the Christian religion—belong to science as much as the facts of chemistry or physics. Those facts are not so much what the Bible records, as the observed effects of religion on human life. About the Bible stories there may be and always will be dispute, but about the effects of religion on contemporary life—on character, on conduct, for health, for illumination—something like certain conclusions should be reached.

Belief is a fact. What you believe may not all be true, but that you believe it is a fact. The effects of belief and of conduct affected by it are facts. If religion enlightens the mind; induces love, sanity, patience, forbearance; cures disease both mental and physical—all those things are facts which science, or the newspapers, or any observing person, may record and study. If religion is good for mankind and the world, especially in the present crisis, there must be and are accessible facts to prove it, and whenever they are observed with due intelligence it should be determinable what in current religion does good and what does evil. People work too much with theory in religion, and not enough with fact. They talk too much about what it claims to do and ought to do, and not enough about what it does. Science has quit that method. It tests every theory by fact and trusts no theory except as its facts support it. No doubt the weakness of religion in our day is that its facts have not sufficiently supported its theories and claims. Its great facts—its great results—are in the lives of men, and they may not have been good enough in our time to give people the confidence in Christianity as a world saver that it deserves.

So much the more valuable, now, are all facts which make for confidence in religion, and in its power to rescue the world from its present plight. The very pith and essence of religion is the belief in an invisible world to which our visible and material world is related by the closest ties, and out of which it is possible to get help in the solution of our earthly problems. That is the sort of help we need for the Washington conference, and the call for universal prayer at the opening of it was an instinctive recognition that that help is needed. We want spiritual assistance. So much anybody of intelligence will admit. Anybody who thinks will concede that materialism has made a mess of the job of managing this world and that we need an infusion of what might be called spiritualism into the management, if we are to salvage what is left. But where do they expect to get their spiritualism—their spirituality? Is it a product of the material and visible world that they are so concerned about? No; it isn't! It is a product of the spiritual and invisible world, about which so many good and valuable people have only vague and timorous ideas, and no belief positive enough to accomplish what they would. They want spirituality—something to temper the selfishness of men, but the price of it is belief— an urgent, practical belief in a spiritual and invisible source of the spirituality that they want, and they cannot pay that price. They have not got it.

But there are those who have it, and they are, as usual, the hope of the world, and should be the best helpers of the conference. It is they, perhaps, who can furnish its inspiration. Our life here is largely an exercise in dealing with material things, and to do that successfully, even with all the spiritual assistance we can get, takes all our brains and much knowledge. The conference has predominantly to deal with material things, and we all have confidence that its membership includes possessors of all the knowledge and experience necessary to that duty. The office of people, in the churches or out, whose belief is vivid and practiced enough to get help out of the invisible world, is to bring the conference that help. It will surely need it; it is likely to win or lose according as it gets it or not; and, since the world has need that the conference should win something effectual, let all helpers help with all they know and all they can.

Miss Jane Addams went to the League sittings at Geneva and reported when she came away that the League needed humanizing. So will the conference need humanizing, and it is the office of all of us—of the mass of interested people—to humanize it every day all we can. If it is to be a success, it must be a popular success. It cannot be a success of specialists. Whatever it achieves that is good must in the main be an achievement of human hearts. We may best keep Christmas this

year by "rooting" for that conference, sustaining
it, feeling its importance, helping it by mind, by
will, by soul, by speech, and written word in so
far as we can. There is a great chance for it, and,
gracious! what a need! What difficulties confront it—Japan sensitive, aspiring, only a couple
of generations from feudalism, instructed mainly
in those methods of the Western civilization that
were finally scrapped, we all hope, by the War.
How will the conference think with Japan, feel
with Japan, give Japan a fair deal, and yet do its
duty not only by Europe and America, but by
Asia? Japan is difficult, but, after all, Japan is
human and the conference must be humanized
enough to find her humanity. Everything that
conference must do is difficult. France is difficult, and Germany, and all middle Europe, and
the limitation of armament, and perhaps there will
even be something to say about Ireland. Its dance
is an egg dance. The more reason why we should
all help it by all the means we can, mental and
spiritual, hand and voice and printed word.

Our best hopes for the conference and for any
radical improvement in the methods of conducting
human life on this planet are, frankly, religious
hopes, based on the birth we celebrate at Christmas, and the ministry and the teachings that followed. If there is not enough in Christianity to
save our present edifice of civilization—enough
wisdom, enough illumination, enough power—then
the outlook is far from bright, for other means
have been tried repeatedly in past ages, and there

are only ruins to show for the civilizations they could not save.

No, not ruins only; but besides them an imperfect record of experiences. We know, in a way, the course those earlier civilizations ran and through what processes they crumbled. In that knowledge we ought to be wiser than our fathers, and there is hope that we are. Besides all the pages of history, we have vividly before our eyes the spectacle of a war surpassing in destructiveness any that we have record of, and proceeding out of very much such circumstances and rivalries as those that destroyed in turn the civilizations that preceded ours. We know more clearly and more generally than was ever known before what lies ahead for us and all we have, if we cannot mend the ways of human life. We see limitless knowledge within our grasp if civilization can hold together long enough for us to attain it. We see destruction awaiting the present works of man if that growing knowledge takes destructive forms. We know what our case is and some of us know there is a cure for it. In the Washington conference there is a means to make that cure practically operative. It belongs to us to feel, then, that all that we can do to make that conference successful is done to save our civilization from what befell Egypt, Assyria, the Roman Empire, and all the rest.

The Girls

MAY 1922

NE HEARS THAT THE GIRLS ARE OUT OF hand. The newspapers take notice of it; also the gossips. People who have children who have reached the disorderly age, say between seventeen and twenty-five, know more or less what the other young people of that age are about, and report on it, very privately when it concerns their own children, but as to other people's children with a proper candor. They say the girls are bolder than they should be—forward in their attentions to young men, and obstreperously indifferent to what used to be considered propriety. Maybe there is still propriety, but we are assured that it is a different article, a different standard, from what it was ten years ago. There is argument anent it all, whether the girls are better or worse than their grandmothers, and the argument that they are better by no means lacks supporters who maintain that one must not judge them by externals, since some of the least restrained of them are all right at heart and very promising guardians for the generation to come.

Well, we hope so. We hope for the best about everything in this world and keep on hoping. When things do not improve we optimists say, "Of course, they must be worse before they are better," and when they get worse we rate that as a sign of coming improvement. And indeed we are quite justified in not being overalarmed about the girls, because they are going to keep on with us, no matter what happens, if we keep on ourselves. They cannot be abolished by amending the Constitution. As an institution they are clear away above the law—something fundamental and superhuman and any other powerful and comprehensive word you think of. When we talk about their behavior, it is as though we discussed freckles or something else that comes and goes.

All the same, we may consider whether women in our day are on the right job, and, if not, what can be done to conduct them to it. Some day there will be a discussion whether suffrage has affected them at all, and, if it has, whether it has done them good or harm; also it will be discussed whether woman suffrage has had an effect on our world, and, if it has, whether it has made it better or worse. But these discussions are not yet. Everything that happens now that people do not like they blame on the War, and you could not yet untangle the effects of the War on women from the effects of the vote on them. Possibly both the vote and the War did them good. I guess they did, and that these ructionary manners of the young ones are just accompanying stages to improvement. New liberty always does some damage to the liberated. It is intoxicating, and not all heads can stand it, nor all legs.

I have not the hardihood to imagine taking away the vote from women who have had it, but I can imagine their throwing it back on our hands as something not worth their while; and indeed it is argued that it is not worth their while. The learned Doctor Jacks of Oxford, who edits the *Hibbert Journal*, might take that view, for votes mainly concern government, and Doctor Jacks thinks that the public interest of all nations is far more intensely centered on government than government is worth. In an article contributed the other day to the New York *Evening Post*, he said:

The need of "government," though unquestionably real, is not the primary need of mankind, and all attempts to make it so are doomed to defeat themselves to the end of time. Man's primary need is for light, and until this is recognized, and made into a new basis of human relationship, the world will continue to advance from bad to worse on the path of confusion and strife.

It is a familiar charge that man has always put on woman all the drudgery he could. The vote was to emancipate her, but, perhaps, after all, man, when he handed it to her with so polite a bow, was merely up to his old tricks of putting off on her something he was tired of doing himself, and something that had ceased to be of first importance. Perhaps man is secretly and instinctively of Doctor Jacks's opinion about government—that it is not so important as some other things, and expects gradually to put it off on the sex that is strongest in dealing with details, and go off himself after those other things, and especially, as Doctor Jacks suggests, after light. The trouble about that is that a large proportion of

the new light seems to come through women—
that it appears not to be intended that man should
get anywhere by himself. Where there is a Dante
there is a Beatrice. It is not recorded who filled
that office for Roger Bacon, who seems to have got
an unusual line of information from some source
or other, and apparently out of his own head. But
Beatrice was most helpful to Dante after she had
died, and that leaves a door open for assistance to
Roger Bacon which might not be less feminine
because it was invisible. And there was Joan
of Arc through whom help came to France, working for the most part through very stupid men.

BUT now again about the girls. Accepting the
hypothesis that they are disorderly, what is
the cure for it? Is it the trouble that the mothers
are neglecting their duties—that discipline is slack?
It may very well be in the more extreme cases that
the mothers are no better than they should be, and
have, themselves, relaxed standards of morality or
decorum, and it may be in some cases that good
mothers, who knew their duty toward their daughters, have not been able to do it because the license
of the times ran too strong against them. In all
things the spirit of these times is against compulsion. The War brought an immense enlargement
of liberty. In this country it sent thousands of the
best-born and the best-brought-up girls out into
comparatively unguarded public service—in many
cases beyond the seas. There had been no like
emancipation of young women from restraint since

our fathers migrated to this country. Affairs were
running strong toward increased liberty for young
women for years before the War. The girls' colleges were nurseries of that movement. When the
War came it fairly went over the top, and the girls
that came along immediately after the War are thoroughly infected with it. People who think that
mothers will regain the control of daughters which
they had a generation ago must anticipate a much
greater reaction in things in general than most of
us can see the signs of. Government by mothers
is important, just as all government is important,
but as to domestic government, the case is very
much the same as with political government, which
Doctor Jacks says is not so important as it seems
because the vital need is the need of light. The
thing that is going to help the girls is not so much
rules and authority, though some of them need
both, as understanding of life. If they can be
helped to that, the help will amount to something.

That, I take it, is the light which Doctor Jacks
calls for—understanding of life. The whole world
needs it; the girls need it because they are a part
of the contemporary world and subject to its impulses and distresses. Being at a time of life
when emotion runs strong and experience has not
yet gathered much power of regulation, they show
more visibly than older people the symptoms of
the world disease, and, being girls, their deviations
from decorum seem to observers more scandalous
and disquieting than if they were men. Yet the

men, the gunmen, for example, show even more astonishing deviations. In their remarkable behavior the girls are seekers after understanding of life—the same quest that Doctor Jacks would put us all on when he says that the world's great need is light. The light it needs is something that will illuminate our adventure on earth and help us to understand it and to handle it better, with more intelligence and with more success. When one says that what the world needs is religion, that is the same story in different words. It means that we need a truer understanding of life and it directs us to religion to get it. If we do not get it out of religion, then religion does not help us.

Winston Churchill, the American novelist, who has devoted three years to efforts to come to a better understanding about life, and has begun to disclose his findings, says, "Religion must give you creative energy or it is nothing." His quest is to get something out of religion that will give people increased power over their own lives, over their behavior, over their happiness. That is the most important quest that human minds are following to-day, and many of them are pursuing it, and not without promise of arriving somewhere. That serious observer, Herbert Croly, the leading editor of the *New Republic*, contributed a long discourse to that paper in February on "Behaviorism in Religion," the gist of which was that the world must have a better understanding of human life and that it was likely to get it through religion if religion and science could be induced to work together.

Science, he thought, had at last come far enough toward understanding what sort of a creature man is, and what his ingredients are, and what are the influences that affect him, to verify and illuminate the conception of man and of human relations that appears in the sayings of Christ in the New Testament.

"Modern civilization," Mr. Croly said, "is cracking for want of a religious truth which can earn the allegiance of men by its ability, if voluntarily accepted, to liberate and integrate human life. Christianity claims to possess this virtue and might possess it if the Christian ministry can reach a common interpretation of their faith. . . . Formidable as the task is, we believe the Christian ministry can undertake it with a sufficient chance of success if only they will adjust their minds to its necessity. Their chance of success is born of the profound congruity between the conception of human nature revealed by Jesus Christ two thousand years ago and the conception of human nature which is now obtaining year by year, as the result of scientific investigation, increasing authority and acquiescence."

That is almost as much as to say that science has almost discovered that the Sermon on the Mount is a practical treatise on human relations, which is comforting as far as it goes, and interesting, too. What is not so comforting is the suggestion that the power of Christianity to liberate and integrate human life is dependent on the ability of the Christian ministry to reach a common interpretation of their faith. If Christianity can't operate until its ministers get together it's a bad case, and fit to persuade stock operators to sell the market. But why wait for them? Did gravitation wait for concurrence of scientists with Newton's theory? Gravitation is a law that works without regard for contemporary opinion, but people who understand it have an advantage over people who don't. If Christianity also is a law, that will work also without much regard to the opinions of ministers, and people who understand it and use it will benefit by it without deference to the ministers' feelings. No one has a patent on Christianity. The world, after some centuries of hesitation, has pretty much accepted that position, and actions for infringement are no longer dangerous.

Mr. Croly seems to hope to see religion so exhibited that the scientific mind can grasp and understand it, and to see science so expounded that the religious mind may get out of it a confirmation of what it has received by spiritual intelligence. That seems very much what Mr. Winston Churchill is driving at. "We can," he says, "with the help of modern science, in biology and psychology, reach a theory as to the nature of the mind that will account for man's dualism, the conflict between emotions. Each of us has a body that is torn by mental conflicts. The problem is to resolve them. We are on the way toward finding out what the source of all our neuroses is to-day, and when we have done that we will liberate powers undreamed of. Morality has crumbled simply

because we do not understand what religion really
means. We are entitled to a scientific explanation
of the forces operating in us, and there has been
none. But I am sure that it can be put in terms
of modern science, and when that has been done
we will know how to put an end to the mental conflicts that now rage in everyone's being, crippling
the power that exists in each of us, and will learn
how to use our mental energy as we should."

These are still obscure matters about which
most of us have very limited understanding. We
pick up an idea here and an idea there, and the most
that most of us have learned as yet is that there is
something to be found out which, if we can discover
it, will be helpful to human conduct, to international
politics, to the behavior of girls, and the dealings of
nations one with another. Compulsion, as said, is
pretty well recognized as a broken reed in human
affairs. It accomplishes only momentary things. If
it dams a flood the waters run over the top of the
dam, or if they do not it merely puts things back and
postpones solutions that are due. The world main-
tains its police forces to keep things from getting
too much out of hand, and that seems right, but it
never looked so little to compulsion for solutions.
In that particular it seems to be getting around
to the New Testament view of human life and
the way to deal with it—the view that Mr. Croly
says the scientists begin to see the point of. The
hope of the world nowadays is not in armies or in
navies, not even in the elimination of war by

chemistry; it is in thought and the better understanding of life; in the acceptation of knowledge
and the infusion of credibility into many things
that have been incredible. That is the job of
science—to make the incredible credible; to make
the incomprehensible understandable; to increase
belief, especially in scientists, and confirm the religious people in all the truth they have and detach
them from such error as is mixed with it. If you
think all that is going on while we wait, it makes
the prospects of this troubled world seem a good
deal better, and encourages everyone to live on a
few years more and see how things work out,
whereas for folks who feel that the very difficult
complications that the Great War has left in its
wake must all be brought to solution without any
new helps to thought or action, the prospect must
be considerably enveloped with haze. Happily
for our world, it is full of forward-looking people
who expect it to outlast all its troubles, and whom
the recognition of difficulties only confirms in confidence in the ability of man to overcome them, and
in faith that all the power he needs to that end exists and is waiting for him to recognize and use it.

A World That Needs Saving

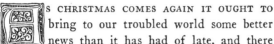S CHRISTMAS COMES AGAIN IT OUGHT TO bring to our troubled world some better news than it has had of late, and there is a prospect that it will. Europe in matters economic has improved, but in matters political has seemed to be going from bad to worse for many months. There are times when one says things must be worse before they can be better, and that rather gloomy suggestion has been the mainstay of observers who hope for better things. Things political got suddenly worse when the Kemalist Turks thrashed the Greeks and captured Smyrna, which was burned in consequence, leaving hundreds of thousands of homeless refugees. Then came the advance of the Turks to the neutral zone of the Dardanelles, the resistance of the British, and the general taking of counsel which is going on at this writing, with the results still uncertain but promising.

So perhaps that worse, which must precede betterment, has happened. One thing that makes it look so is the disturbance in the minds of the organized churches in the United States at the massacres, killings, burnings, and deportations that have attended the Turkish advance. The church people in this country, with something like general accord, have remonstrated at the failure of our

government to take effective measures in depreca-
tion of these doings. The newspapers have reported that the State Department and the White
House were flooded with remonstrances. Why
aren't you doing something? the church people asked
Secretary Hughes, and his answer was that he
had done all that he had power to do, and that
the only way to do more was to get more power
from Congress. That brought home to many minds
afresh and with energy the drawbacks of the policy
of isolation from the affairs of Europe. It can
be argued, and it is argued, that the whole Turkish
uprising is a consequence of the absence of the
United States from the counsels of Europe, an
absence that dates from the rejection of the Treaty
of Versailles by the Senate. Over and over again
we have been assured that the recovery of Europe was doubtful and would certainly be long
deferred if the United States did not help about
it. Month after month we have seen that assurance coming true—France and England, rivals for
power and squabbling in their rivalry; Germany
driven toward bankruptcy, and now the Turks
taking advantage of the discord among the late
Allies to renew political pretenses that the War
had seemed to quench for all time. Europe has
drifted along; we have drifted along. Suddenly
come these Turkish massacres and the American
churches seem to wake up and want something
done.

Another important group wants something done.
The bankers at this writing are holding a great

meeting in New York. The most important message that is brought to that meeting and distributed from it over the United States is that we must bear our share of the troubles of Europe and help to cure them, and in that opinion the bankers and the church people seem to be of one mind. They both want to save the world, the church people for spiritual reasons, the bankers, perhaps, because they have lent money on it; though many of the bankers are pious men, and spiritual reasons have weight with them too.

All this news of a growing agitation of the public mind in very important groups in the United States on the subject of our relations with Europe and our duty to the Eastern hemisphere, is good news. If enough Americans realize that this country must do something, something will be done. There are people who have thought that Europe and Asia were no concerns of ours; that their misfortunes were their own fault, and that with power to help them we were justified in holding back and leaving them to reap the harvest of their infirmities. But we are not justified in any such course. In so far as we have the power to help and do not use it, we may expect our own system to be poisoned. It is by helping others that we best help ourselves. That is true in business, in banking and in all the work of the church. It is even true in politics, which is nothing more than the governmental end of all these other activities.

A great wave of revolution is sweeping through the world and preparing it for new things. To

block it is impossible, but to check and guide it is
feasible if we all take hold. The work of revolution is mainly destructive. If it goes too far,
the good and the bad go down together in the
crash. Revolution in the present world has gone
about far enough. It is time to save the pieces of
civilization before the whole fabric is destroyed, and
for that work the appeal is to the United States
beyond any existing nation.

Listen to the closing words of the speech of
Mr. Thomas Lamont to the assembled bankers on
October 3d in New York. He talked about the
state of Europe politically "in the wilderness,"
economically better because the people were at work
raising crops and saving money. Then he considered international debts, and especially the ten
billion dollars and more that was owing to the
United States. Of that sum he said about one
half was lent to the Allies after we entered the
War. We could not send troops, but we sent
money, and gave large credits for war material
and supplies. Mr. Lamont did not say that this
part of the debts due us should be canceled, but
that was evidently his opinion. He invited the
bankers to think about this five billions from us
that went into the War after it had become our war,
and consider what should be done about it.

A part of the debt due to us, he said, could
never be paid, and as to that he did not hesitate
to say it should be canceled. Of what was col-
lectible some time or other, he made that distinction between the debts incurred before we got into

the War and those incurred after we got in.   Undoubtedly, it was Mr. Lamont's opinion, as a banker
and as a patriot, that Europe's obligations to us
should be scaled down, and not from sentimental
motives but because it was the part of wisdom and
of sound banking, sound politics, and sound business to lighten the burdens of Europe so far as we
could.   He said finally:

Do not forget that as the nations of Europe face great
dangers America too is facing a crisis, though of a different
order.   We have gained great power.   With the power goes
weighty responsibility.   Have we discharged it?   For the
period of the world war my answer is yes, a thousandfold yes.
For the period since the armistice can any one of us search his
heart and answer yes?   We have, it is true, offered criticism to
the nations of Europe.   We have shouted advice across to
them.   But we have been timid and fearful of petty entangle-
ments.   Now we have, it would seem, come to the parting of
the ways.   Shall we meet the responsibility that has come
with our power or shall we fail?   Shall you and I give our mind,
our understanding and our sympathy to these problems or
shall we stand aside and add to our national stock of gold?
Shall we urge upon our National Government active co-operation in the counsels of the Mother Country and of the Old
World?   Or shall we keep silent?
    Nineteen hundred years ago there was One who said: "For
unto whomsoever much is given of him shall much be required."   And again He said: "With what measure ye mete,
it shall be measured to you again."   What shall we measure
for ourselves?   Shall it not once more be the courage that is
America's tradition?   Shall it not be the generosity as well
as the justice that, among all the nations of the earth, will
in truth and name make America first?

No sounder message than that to the American
people can come from anyone, and no more fitting

message for the Christmas season. If we believe in peace on earth, we must believe also in good will to men. There is plenty of it in this country; the problem is to get it moving and give it wise direction. The church people are useful agents in getting it going: in present circumstances the bankers may be very useful agents in giving it right direction. When the church organizations stormed the State Department in clamors to fight the Turks, their feelings did them credit but their energies were not directed to the right spot. Europe can handle the Turks if the nations of Western Europe can get together. The great errand of the United States is to help them to harmony; to help them to put aside national contentions and work together to save the civilization of Europe. If we can help them appreciably by scaling down the debts they owe us, that seems to be the first step that we should take. We can help them still further and perhaps still more by entering their counsels and being represented by competent delegates in discussions that concern the management of the world.

The last seems to means that in some way or other we should get into the League of Nations, the organization that in these days is the sanest and most useful council that Europe affords. Of course that is a hard task. We tried to get into the League and our effort fell through. It has been proposed lately that we might enter it as we entered the War, not as an ally but as an associate. When we went into the War we were not bound by any of the inter-Ally treaties. Our errand was simply to help win the War by any means we could. We bargained for nothing, we demanded nothing. That position worked very well in the War. If we went into the League of Nations on the same basis, we might be useful there again. That is a detail proper for discussion; a plan that may be good or may not. But somehow we must be quit of isolation.

It all comes to this, that our greatest Christmas obligation this year is to the world beyond our borders. We have plenty to do at home; we always do have, but our home duties and our foreign duties are all tied up together and we cannot do justice to either if we neglect the other.

The great thing the world needs, as always, but pre-eminently this year, is religion: the understanding and application of the great Christmas message. All the great problems before it—reparations, international debts, participation in the councils of the League, strikes, labor problems, and farmers' profits are full of thorny possibilities. The temper in which they are approached is everything, and that temper depends upon the ideas about human life, its purpose and conditions, that are in the minds of the men who confer. The materialists—the people who believe that men can live by bread alone, and that more bread and more of other material accessories is the great aim of human effort—will never bring peace to earth. That great achievement, in so far as it is ever accomplished, will be the work of a different order of minds, of the minds that put spiritual things—

righteousness, courage, justice, kindness, love—
above all the material things, and believe that if
they can attain and possess the spiritual valuables,
the other necessaries will be added to them. The
great thing that is going on in the world now is
the demonstration that that idea of life that puts
spiritual things before material things is sound; that
not only good morals depend upon it, but good
business and the welfare of states and people.
There is an old saw, "Be good and you will be
happy," but what all the world is finding out now
is that it cannot be happy unless it is good, and
that it cannot make up for lack of goodness by
any kind of advantage it may procure by strength
or wiles.

And goodness implies, not merely correct deportment, not merely observance of the law and
impeccable morals, but good will and helpfulness
and the courage to take responsibilities that belong
to one. The neutral kind of good will, which
merely lets things alone, is not enough in these
days. What is needed, and what at this season
and this year the circumstances of all the world
demand from the United States, is that more positive good will that sees a need, that assumes a
duty, and helps for the sake of helping, without
too keen an eye for immediate profit or loss, but
with the conviction that true prosperity for any
nation can only come out of service to its neighbors.

The Pith of Religion

IT IS DISPUTED, I BELIEVE, WHETHER TIME really exists, the understanding of the super-informed being that Time is no more than a sort of habit of the human mind. All the same the clocks and other devices measure it and the habit goes on. The years succeed one another and are numbered as they pass under the wire, and here's a new one coming in now.

Twenty-three is not a lucky number. The prejudice against it is not so strong as against thirteen, but in sporting circles, at least, it is not well thought of. We take the years, however, as they come and make the best we can of them. Expectations for 1923 are not very brilliant. The stage has not yet been set for a golden year. There is a lot to do before the world can be even normally happy, and throughout this year that is about to start, we shall probably be busy doing some of those things rather than merely enjoying life. The relations of the nations must continue to be mediated; something must be done about the finances of Europe; there will be a lot more starving people standing in line. We start out with a coal shortage but that may not be serious. To have much to do is not in itself a bad outlook at New Year's because the doing of things that should be done brings happiness, and perhaps we shall have

some of that kind of happiness. It is the kind
we ought to have if we are to have any.

The other day a high Court in California gave
out a decision that the King James version of the
Bible, being the book "of a certain sect," cannot
be read in the public schools of California. That
seems unfortunate because not to know the Bible
is a serious defect in education. It is too bad about
the Bible that it makes so much trouble. Headlines in the paper almost every day disclose that
this or that clergyman has incurred or achieved
publicity by an opinion about something in the
Bible which other clergymen object to. There is a
row in the Presbyterian Church over the opinions
of the Rev. Harry Emerson Fosdick of New York.
There is a row in the Methodist Church in Ne-
braska over Parson Buckner, who thinks that certain statements about God in the Old Testament
are not so. There is the row between Mr. Bryan
and many supporters over the supposed conflict
between the theory of evolution and the Book of
Genesis. There is the row between the Fundamentalists, who insist apparently upon belief in the
literal inspiration of the whole Bible from cover to
cover as it stands, and the Progressives who are
for the catch-as-catch-can method of Bible reading,
and who would have readers believe only so much
as they think is true. Really, to clear up our con-
flicting notions about the Bible is a highly important piece of work. It has a bearing upon the peace
of the world and the progress as well as the com-
posure of human life, and deserves to be included

among the big jobs that should engage our wits in
1923. For the world needs religion; that is all
but universally admitted; and the basis of the
religion which Christendom knows best and most
relies on is the Bible.

Now what is the nature of the difficulties about
the Bible? It is that it contains statements which,
taken literally, seem to conflict with accepted current knowledge. Mr. Bryan is concerned because
he cannot make the literal text of Genesis conform
with his notions of Darwinism. Stars above!
What's the hurry? Can't he see what Genesis is?
Can't he see what Darwin's theory is? If he
thinks they conflict, can't he wait for more light
before insisting that they shall get together? There
are millions of pious people for whom the apparent
disparities between Genesis and Darwinism make
no trouble at all. Perhaps they understand the
kind of literary conglomerate that Genesis is; perhaps they understand the tentative quality of the
theory of evolution. Perhaps they don't. But,
anyhow, they are perfectly content to let truth
work out. Their conduct in this life and their
hopes in a life hereafter do not in the least depend
upon any premature welding together of Darwinism and Genesis.

Take Parson Buckner's difficulty about the dealings of the Israelites with the Canaanites. It per-
plexes him because he reads in the Old Testament
that God instructed the Israelites to clean up the
Canaanites, man, woman, and child. He does
not feel that God, being a good God, gave

them any such instructions, and surely he is entitled to entertain that sentiment. But God is a very large idea, which our human consciousness cannot measure with any tape line that is yet at its command. The "and God said" of the Old Testament books seems very like a detail of phraseology, which expressed the sense of the Israelite leaders, however derived, that the Canaanites were a bad lot, with whom the chosen people must not be mixed up either in race or religion. Parson Buckner may be right about what "God said" in the Old Testament, but surely he can be either right or wrong without impairing his value as an expositor of the teachings of Christ. Ministers are expected, while they are still young at the threshold of their profession, to accept a lot of assertions about the Bible that it takes a lifetime often to understand. It is not really necessary that they should do it. The beliefs that they must have, if they are to be useful ministers, are few and simple.

The ministerial employment seems nowadays to have two branches, one of them concerned with spiritual matters and the other with organization and its fruits as they appear in what we call good works. The aim of organization seems to be largely to take care of people's material needs. That branch of the ministerial employment is concerned a good deal with raising money and spending it. The other branch has to do with quite a different matter—with reaching into the invisible world and drawing out of it strength and direction for human

life, and that is a very personal adventure to which
organization can be only supplementary. Both of
these labors, of course, are important, but this last
office is the great function of the ministry. Religion is the tie that binds the visible to the invisible
world. The pith of religion is the belief in immortality. The practice of religion has to do with
the relief of material human needs, but for the
spirit that incites us to succor the widows and
the fatherless, the needy and the sick, and to foster
the increase of knowledge, we are instructed to go
to the great source of charity and understanding
in the invisible world. The church by its existence, by its service, by its institutions helps us to
do that. It gives us assurance that the invisible
world is accessible to us, that there is help for us
there if we will seek it. And so it helps, or should
help, us to get a better understanding of our relations with men and a better intelligence in dealing
with them. Those are the things the world now
most needs—more than food, more than clothes,
more than relief of any kind, though the need of
these in many countries is still bitter beyond all
precedent. It needs understanding of life, understanding of our fellow men, and an inspired intelligence in putting ourselves in their places and
dealing with them as we should wish to be dealt
with.

The office of the Bible is to help to give us that
understanding of life. We get it mainly from the
New Testament, of which the Old Testament is the
background, and, to us Christians, mainly valu-

able in that capacity. We do not, as Christians, profess to get our standards of conduct from the Old Testament, or shape our deportment on the behavior of the Israelites. We are not excused for anything we do because the Israelites did it. They are not the example we profess to follow. That example is in the New Testament. Accordingly, we have no serious occasion to worry about what seems to us misconduct in the Children of Israel, or about the locutions their historians used in recording their exploits. Still, the Old Testament is very interesting in showing us how folks behaved in Asia some centuries ago, and what sort of religion they had, and New Testament and Old are alike in recording a steady, operating, and inspiring belief in the invisible world, and that is one of the vastly important matters to understanding of which the Bible gives invaluable help.

Current spiritism is trying hard to help us in that same field of exploration, but it labors under difficulties. It is not very respectable and the godly are apt to shy at it, whereas the Bible, as an institution, is respectability enthroned, and what it says goes with the godly if they can be made to understand it. But weird and scary as modern spiritism is, there are those who think it the most interesting and probably the most important activity now proceeding in the world. It has spread remarkably. It is going on in many countries. It gets a wary and usually skeptical attention from some of the scientists. People of good minds, good character, and good training are in-

terested in it more and more. Even some of the
ministers take notice of it, though as a rule they
are still shy of meddling with it, and watch it from
afar off. That is natural enough because the old
spiritualism that blazed out seventy years ago,
came down to our generation considerably be-
smirched. It was noticed abundantly, but never
got due examination by qualified people nor was
geared to any working plan for helping human
life, so that while it did not pass away, it did
pass out of public notice. The present recurrence
of interest in communication with the dead and
with the invisible world is put down as a fruit of
the War. People say that, and seem to think that
they have explained it, and that we should expect
that when the other effects of the War have passed
away finally, the interest in these things will go
with them. And so in some measure it may, but
even if it does, there may be a work for it to
do first, a work of the first importance, no less than
to revitalize belief in the Christian religion—to
give it new power, to bring home to men an understanding of life, to make them feel why they are
in this world and what is their great employment
here, and by what means they may find the knowledge and inspiration to discharge it.

What mankind needs more than anything else
is spiritual knowledge. We are getting knowledge
fast, wonderfully fast, but most of it is applied to
material things. In the last two generations the
power of man over material things has enormously
increased. The alarming feature of the late war

was that the developments of science had made man
so strong materially that the collapse of civilization was threatened. It is still threatened. Another great war, as we all know, would probably
be more destructive than the last and how much of
the machinery of life it would leave nobody can
tell, not even the bankers. In the face of this
greatly increased power of destruction, we need
an increased power of salvation, and that must be
a spiritual power. The mental side of man has
been developed for two generations while his spiritual side has been starved. What is needed now
is a development of that spiritual side so that it
will hold the rest of the new knowledge and make
it safe.

Most of the knowledge of spiritual things which
the world possesses is credited to revelation; that
is, it came out of the invisible world and was given
to our world through living men. The Bible is
full of such communications from cover to cover.
The Christian religion is based on such communications. If they are coming now it is nothing that
should be repugnant to Christian thought. If from
people and from powers and from teachers in the
invisible world, thoughts and purposes and guidance and instruction are communicated to living
people here, it need not astonish unduly any Christian who reads his Bible. The question for him is
whether the fact of communication is true and
whether the matter communicated is valid and
useful.

Even in religion it seems important that we

should get the news. The ministers have not
been getting it all, and it is worth their reverend
attention. If they get it more fully there will be
more ministers with messages of power, more ministers with confidence in the vital teachings of the
Bible. But their messages must be true or they are
nothing; and how difficult it is to sort the truth out
of the news, may be learned by reading the newspapers.

But the scientists are going to help. They want
the news, but even more they want the truth.
They are not quite so closely tied to accepted beliefs as the ministers are, and can take greater
chances in speculation. What they learn about
nature and about man is a part of that great body
of truth which includes all religion, and which is
making it possible to understand details of knowledge that could hardly have been understood one
thousand or two thousand years ago. We can
only accept what our minds have been prepared to
accept. It seems that nowadays our minds are
being made ready for extraordinary new acquisi-
tions of knowledge and of spiritual knowledge most
of all, for that is most important and is the frame-
work on which everything hangs. To get the news
that is important—the spiritual news as well as
the rest; to follow truth wherever it leads and from
whatever source it emanates—those are the attrac-
tions for aspiring minds; and it is the aspiring
minds, the minds that see visions and can interpret
them and put their messages into practice, which

the church above all institutions needs and will profit by.

Given knowledge enough and minds free to work, and the difficulties about the Bible will fade away. Readers will go to it more than ever to learn the lesson of life, for confirmation of suggestions they get from other quarters, for assurance that knowledge and developments that seem new are old truths which have been more or less in the world since before recorded history, which sink out of sight at times, or are driven into hiding by intolerance or persecution, but come out again when suffering and distress have made them necessary to the world and sent seekers to find them.

The Bible is a wonderful book, the most important book we have. All the stupidities, extravagances, and timidities of its various guardians cannot kill it; much less can the assaults of its assailants. But it takes some intelligence to get out what is in it, and make some of the old knowledge that it contains harmonious with the new knowledge which we get from putting the works of God under the microscope and examining them in laboratories, and by studying rocks, and digging up bones and old manuscripts and deciphering old inscriptions. A sort of inspired intelligence is needed to produce that harmony, but the inspiration will be forthcoming. The thing for us to be concerned about is that the intelligence shall be free; that men who think shall not be scared out of their thoughts, whether or not they match the thoughts of other men who happen to be in authority.

Government

F ONE READS THE NEWSPAPERS FAITH-
fully, he must conclude that the world
is not making a running start of it in its
race toward the new era. On the contrary, it is
laboring profoundly. The clouds above it are
very black, so black as to make our Ambassador at
London observe that the condition of Europe has
become immeasurably worse in the last two years
and that if it had to go through another year
like those, he did not know what would happen to
it or to any of us. So he said at a public dinner.
He is not a gloomy man like Dean Inge. When
he takes so dark a view of things it sounds quite
solemn, even though he suggests that it may be
the darkness before the dawn.

And so it may. Something has got to break in
Europe, and it may be those clouds. It is a common condition of improvement that things should
get worse. That condition has been steadily and
progressively met during the last two years. Europe as managed by its governments has justified
the sentiment of a former ambassador to London,
who wrote in a letter in December, 1915: "The
sheer stupidity of governments is amazing. They
are all so human; so very human. I would not be
a government for any earthly consideration. I'd
rather be a brindled dog and trot under a wagon."

Walter Page, when he wrote that, had been through a year and a quarter of the War, and was in intimate relations with all the nations engaged in it. Besides being the London agent for the United States, which was enough in itself, no doubt, to account for his feelings, he had charge of the embassies of all the Central Powers, and his duties had not left in him a good opinion of government officers. "Of course," he wrote, "everybody is worked to death, but something ails the lot of them all the way from Constantinople to London." And his comment on governments—"They are all so human, so *mighty* human"—carries the implication of frailty, of faultiness, of not being up to the job, and fastens it not merely on the officials, but on the governments they serve. For of course when the world goes to wreck the conclusion that its governments are incompetent is inevitable.

And since the War ended, the best that governments could do has been so far short of being good enough that not without due grounds a contemporary critic notices as one of the most obvious political phenomena of the day the loss of confidence in representative government. Really it is not so gay a pastime as it used to be to govern the nations. When the Greeks the other day shot their unsuccessful generals and the ministers who sent them out, they gave the governmental calling a very rude shock.

A more restrained and even more impressive demonstration of dissatisfaction in government is

the rise of the Fascisti in Italy where a lot of
amateurs have taken the reins away from the pro-
fessionals, pitched them off the box seat, and are
now driving the coach of state. Moreover their
performance is as yet considerably admired. Ke-
mal and his Turks are another lot of interlopers
taking charge successfully when the constituted
authorities had fallen down on their job. Russia
and the Soviets is an appalling example of much
the same thing, and in England since the late
election, the Labor Party, who have never governed, have become His Majesty's Opposition, to
which the King must turn for a new Prime Minister whenever Bonar Law's collection loses its majority in Parliament. We had elections here last
November. The striking thing about them was
the evidence of mutiny against government as it
was. If it had been a presidential election our
government would probably have changed hands.
There seems to be a powerful new impulse all over
the world that most existing governments do not
represent.

It is hardly too much to say that all the considerable governments of the world are in a fair
way to lose their jobs. Our own is no exception.
The Ku Klux is an absurd body, but since the
Fascisti got on top in Italy, it gets its share of
serious examination. The Legion has possibilities, much impaired to be sure by its propensity to
raid the treasury. The farm bloc has numbers
and wants, and a hard-luck story that has the merit
of truth in it. If this country, the least distressed

of all, has organized disturbance on such a scale, is it wonderful that the world in general is coming to be a great cave of Adullam, swarming with the discontented and full of ripening mutinies?

IT IS not hard to attribute most of the major misfortunes of mankind to governments, and to make the imputation look plausible. Except for governments the Great War could not have happened, could it? Governmental rivalries and ambitions brought it on. Except for government and its mistakes there need not have been rebellion in Ireland. Except for misgovernment in Russia Lenin and Trotzky might never have been heard of. Except for governments there could not have developed poison gas and all the new machines of war. Except for governments the farmer bloc, the Legion and the Ku Klux would have no target at which to aim their grievances. It looks as if government was the root of all evil and that the anarchists are right in thinking that the world would do better without it.

But we know better: We know that the real alternative to government is a new government. We know by reading, observation and experience that anarchy is hell and that wherever it bobs up it is the instinct of human beings to contrive a combination, any combination, to beat it. We know that bad government is better than no government and that if bad government is the best we can get we had better put up with that. Government is the thing in sight, the organized power which is

made responsible for the consequences of human
infirmity. "They are all so human," said Page,
"so very human." So they are. So governments
must be. You cannot make them out of anything
but humanity, and humanity is constitutionally
prone to err. The irresponsible combinations that
rise to buck up against governments serve the purpose of communicating ideas, some of which require to be disclosed, but as substitutes for government they are far from engaging. The Ku Klux,
the farmer bloc and the Legion may be some good
for the organization of remonstrance, but would
we trust any one of them with the power to govern us? No. No. Any one of them which got
that power would have to go through a course of
preliminary political training that would take out
of it most of the likeness to what it is now. It is
the merit and the weakness of representative government that in order to continue it must in the
long run be more acceptable to a majority of the
voters than something else. Any government that
suits more than half the voters is bound to be
defective because of the large proportion of fatuity
in the popular support that it rests upon. To sat-
isfy half the voters sufficiently to keep their votes,
the best minds have to make such concessions to
popular preferences as Mr. Wilson made when he
appointed Mr. Bryan as Secretary of State. The
real hope for improvement in government is identical with the hope of improvement in people, and
no people are really safe who have not intelligence

enough to take care of themselves in spite of their governments.

Are we frightened by the Ku Klux—by the farmer bloc—by the acquisitive propensities of the present managers of the Legion? Are we scared because Oregon's extraordinary new school law gives evidence of a purpose to deprive parents of any say about their children's education? Does such a law, following the Eighteenth Amendment and the Volstead law, make us wonder how long any poet will still call these States "the land of the free"? It does make us so wonder undoubtedly, but current organizations for regulative or legislative purposes do not much scare us. They come and go, usually accomplishing something of good as they pass, and disappearing whenever they get to be too gross a nuisance. But government does not so disappear. It is like the vulnerable and ailing physical body of us that holds our soul. Our government never is the soul of the nation, but it is the mechanism through which for some purposes that soul has to work. We know how much trouble we have in making our bodies behave well. We and all nations must expect to have the same sort of trouble with our governments. Just as our bodies can be scared into good habits by sickness, so governments can be scared into the paths of wisdom by the spread of political disease. The Ku Klux and the Oregon school law are symptoms of disease, and so in a way is the farm bloc, but not of a fatal disease. We won't die of it; we won't die of Prohibition. We may be sick but we will get well in due time.

THE great disease that makes trouble just now for all governments is the lack of co-operation among the nations. The people of the world have contrived governments by means of which, faulty as they are, they keep order and get a chance to make their livings. But the nations have not yet been able to accomplish that exploit. They live unprotected except by armies and treaties, and ungoverned except by temporary apprehensions, and variable, unstable and very unequal moral sense. None of them has escaped the consequences of the immensely disturbing and destructive experience which the world has lately gone through. As a family they are in a situation very like what any people would be in without government. Any member at any time is liable to start something that threatens the family's peace, and there is not yet a family council adequate in representation and influence to handle things so started. The League of Nations was invented to do that office and might do it if the United States would come in. We have stood out stubbornly against it. With what consequences? With the result that the world, as our London agent tells us, is immeasurably worse off than it was two years ago, that all governments are falling into disrepute, that our own got an appalling black eye in the late elections, that the farm bloc due to pains caused by lack of buying capacity in Europe threatens us with bad finance, that secret or quasi-secret organizations like the Ku Klux, and class organizations like the Legion, are springing up with intention to compel special and objectionable legislation by terrorizing politicians. The Anti-Saloon League showed how to do it, and what can be done for one purpose may presently be done for ends much less excusable. We would not participate on a reasonable basis in an effort to heal a world disabled by war and torn by factions, and now we face a prospect of being torn by factions ourselves.

In a sense then, things in going very badly are going very well. If a patient won't take his medicine, and doesn't seem to be getting better without it, the best chance for him is to get worse until he comes to a better mind. The medicine that is needed in this detail of the universe is a better line of international co-operation, with the United States an active participant in consultations. The recognition that all governments are bad and some of them awful, but that any government is better than none, might well bring us to more reasonable feelings about the League of Nations. To be sure the League is not a government, not the supergovernment its critics have said it was, but it represents the most definite effort that exists to get the nations out of the wild waste of anarchy. Cut out Article Ten; leave the League without any provision for physical force, and with only moral means of influencing the world; it would still be powerful and still helpful if only it included all the members that ought to belong to it and was imbued with a resolute purpose to do its office. One must not look for perfection in the League, especially to start with. It is more reasonable and more hopeful to think of it, as one must of government, as an objectionable institution, likely to restrict freedom of action, often foolish, usually selfish, but better than anarchy. The purpose of government is not to make people do as they should but to give them a chance to live; not to destroy their individuality but to develop it. The purpose of a central council like the League should be the same; not to impose manners upon the nations but to give them a chance to live; not to destroy nationality, but to give racial talents a chance to develop.

For in spite of the way the world goes and in spite of the fact that when you call the government human, it means disparagement, there are an extraordinary number of people in the world working overtime to save it, and having on the whole more success than they get credit for. Take our own country. The government of it you can read about in the newspapers and call it anything you like, without necessarily implying disrespect to its constituent members, but in the same newspapers you read things every day about the citizens of the country and it makes you wonder how things can go badly with so many people working so hard and so intelligently to make them go right. Even in Europe—most parts of Europe—in spite of the gloomy advices we get, it seems to go better with people than with governments. There are plenty enough good people in the world to keep it going if they have a fair chance. The thing that most of all deprives them of that chance—that cripples them, halts them, puts them back—is war. The true aim of government is not to restrict the liberties of men but to enlarge them by giving them due protection. The true aim of the League is not to restrict the freedom of nations, but to enlarge it by giving them security so that they can divert their energies awhile to the trades, arts and vocations they are good at, and away from soldiering and the production of war material.

But we must help, we must help—we of the United States. M. Clemenceau, though he did not quote Scripture, virtually told us that having put our hand to the plough, we had turned back. That would not do, he said: we must come back to the plough handles.

Old Age Looks Forward

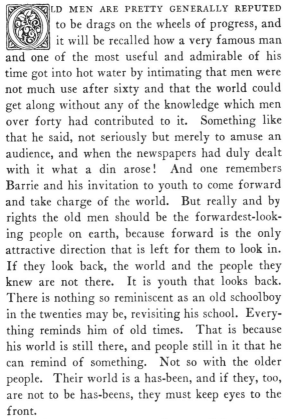LD MEN ARE PRETTY GENERALLY REPUTED to be drags on the wheels of progress, and it will be recalled how a very famous man and one of the most useful and admirable of his time got into hot water by intimating that men were not much use after sixty and that the world could get along without any of the knowledge which men over forty had contributed to it. Something like that he said, not seriously but merely to amuse an audience, and when the newspapers had duly dealt with it what a din arose! And one remembers Barrie and his invitation to youth to come forward and take charge of the world. But really and by rights the old men should be the forwardest-looking people on earth, because forward is the only attractive direction that is left for them to look in. If they look back, the world and the people they knew are not there. It is youth that looks back. There is nothing so reminiscent as an old schoolboy in the twenties may be, revisiting his school. Everything reminds him of old times. That is because his world is still there, and people still in it that he can remind of something. Not so with the older people. Their world is a has-been, and if they, too, are not to be has-beens, they must keep eyes to the front.

Is Clemenceau a has-been? We all know he is

not. The spirit does not age. The body gets more or less old. The mind gets forgetful because, I suppose, it is linked up to the mechanics of the brain, but the spirit is another matter that need not be affected by time. Clemenceau is fairly old, not excessively, but he looks ahead. The thing that interests him is what is going to happen next. If he thinks it won't suit him, he practices to make it suit him better. He is the true countryman of Voltaire who said, "I gave my youth to love but now in my old age I work like the devil." So he did. The old Voltaire worked incessantly and always to make the world better and beat the devils in it and especially the persecutors. As one reads a modern life of him it is astonishing to find how much better he was than the reputation he left to the Nineteenth Century.

My neighbor Maitland, who has progressed toward maturity as far as the later sixties, says it scandalizes him to be so little disturbed at the passing of his contemporaries. If somebody died whom he had always known it used to give him a shock, but now he said, he had had most of the considerable shocks of that sort that were possible, and the lesser ones involving people that were not really part of his life did not jar him as they would once have done. He went to their funerals; he showed respect to their memories; but his real feeling had come to be that to die was all in the day's work, and if the departed had really run their course there was no true objection to departure.

Take your classmates in your college class. The

college class is a unit in the course of man in life which may conveniently be followed. The other night I looked through a book of verses which included a good many read at anniversary meetings of a college class. I made only a short stay with them but long enough to make the discovery above noted, that, contrary to the usual impression we have, youth looks back, whereas age looks around and then forward. There were a lot of poems of occasion in that book and they were retrospective inversely to the years of the poet. It impressed me that the concern about dying grew less and less vocal at every anniversary. The early deaths of men that were favorites were made much of, but as the years went on there was more philosophy and less lamentation, and that all accorded with the facts of life, for when the young die it is contrary to nature, but when the old die it accords with nature. A college class can mourn for its young members prematurely gone, but it cannot pile up cumulative griefs year after year for the leaves that fall in due season from its tree. That would make its reunion with dwindling numbers unbearably lugubrious. It is almost constrained to perceive and acknowledge that life itself is the great university, that death is graduation and funerals the commencement exercises.

So I find that when the time comes when most of our personal investments have been transferred from the insecurities of this life to the speculative interests of the next, there is an increase of the disposition commended by Scripture to let the dead bury their dead, and interest becomes transferred from what is past—people, things, events, everything—to what is still ahead, and includes them all.

Humanity is our great concern. That does not die, does not graduate; at least not yet. Its individuals do, but humanity continues resolutely to avail itself of the schooling of Earth for whatever destiny may await it. And no matter how much our individual years increase or Earth's ties lessen, we cannot lose interest in humanity. We feel, instinctively if not by reason, that it really makes a difference what happens to it. So prone is it to err, so used to disappoint us, that it is always hard to be confident in good hopes for it, but it does seem as if in the period of harsh instruction now proceeding, it were slowly gathering some increase of sense, and some realization that its various families had got to work together for the common good, and that otherwise continued health and due measure of what we call prosperity was not possible for them.

JUST at this writing, though Mr. Hoover has been telling us that the condition of Europe is steadily improving, it does not look so to observers from this continent. France and Great Britain having failed to agree about reparations, France has marched troops into the Ruhr and holds the industrial heart of Germany as security for her dues. The present government of France leans chiefly on force and sees no Germany yet whose word or whose intentions she dares to trust unless she retains the means

to compel Germans to keep their word. That
means big armies, and big armies mean unpro-
ductive expenditure, a prospect and a policy that
has made our government feel that the remnant of
American troops that still lingers on the German
frontier had better come home. When one thinks
of the details of all these matters, the selfish interests in France that fear the restoration of Germany's prosperity, the selfish interest in Germany
that will double and twist in any way to avoid paying even what she can, the selfish interests in Great
Britain that are pinched by the need of markets for
the trade by which they live, the selfish interests of
the United States which see themselves better off
than the rest of the world and wish to keep clear of
all troublesome and possibly expensive complications—the prospect unquestionably looks dubious.
But human life does not much shape itself to
accord with details. On the contrary, details have
to fall in line with the course that human life is
taking. Where that course is toward co-operation,
details may delay but surely cannot block it.
Governments are matters of the moment. One
group of politicians gets control and does what it
sees to do while it has power to do it, and presently
ill luck, the manœuvres of rivals or the pressure of
the facts of life upon the minds of people pitches it
out of office and puts another group in its place.
The ideas that the present government of France
expresses are not permanent ideas. They, and the
activities and hesitations and refusals that result
from them, are merely parts of the great process of

the reshaping of the world. What changes the
world and regulates its course is ideas and the facts
of life. When the ideas don't match the facts, the
ideas have to change, as they have changed and are
still changing in Russia. The great test of governmental and economic ideas is the needs and the
capacity of humanity. The great use of war is to
clear the way for new ideas, the acceptance of which
has become necessary.

Just now the late war is very much disparaged.
It produced enormous inconvenience, bereavement
and destruction; it upset the whole order of life in
some countries; and a large part of that order in
all countries; it disturbed morals; it filled the
world with injured people, and it left behind debts,
damages and pestilent complications galore. That
was a high price to pay for ideas, and there are
those who insist that it was paid in vain. Not so!
The ideas bought at so great price are really in the
world and are really working. That premiers and
ministries and governments balk and disagree is not
so serious as it seems to persons who think that
premiers and governments run the world. Governments have their uses, of course, as also have con-
stitutions, legislatures and laws, and must be; but
they are no more than the instruments by which
music is made audible. When new instruments become necessary they are produced, but the music is
not in the instruments. William James showed
understanding of the source of it when he wrote in
a letter to Mrs. Whitman: "As for me, my bed is
made: I am against bigness and greatness in all

their forms, and with the invisible molecular forces that work from individual to individual, stealing in through the crannies of the world like so many soft rootlets, or like the capillary oozing of water, and yet rending the hardest monuments of man's pride if you give them time. The bigger the unit you deal with, the hollower, the more brutal, the more mendacious is the life displayed. So I am against the big organizations as such, national ones first and foremost; against all big successes and big results; in favor of the eternal forces of truth which always work in the individual and immediately unsuccessful way, underdogs always, till history comes, after they are long dead, and puts them on the top."

Governments do not know yet how strong the adversion to war is. That was one of the lessons of the Great War. They do not know how deep it has gone nor how long it will last. Governments go on and talk and scheme and bluff as though their old weapon of force were still available, but they do not really know what condition it is in, and politicians who are astute are very wary of putting it to the test. France adventures with soldiers to make Germany do certain things, some of which she ought to do, and the rest of us watch her thoughtfully and wonder how her action will strike the neighbors and what the final result of her demonstrations will be. For one thing that has come into the world as the immediate result of the War is an unprecedented distaste for the use of force in politics, and a great doubt as to its value.

Other ideas that have been slowly penetrating the minds of men not only since the War but for the last two generations, have to do with religion and the increased possibilities of power in it. Some of the ideas that have found their most conspicuous expression in Christian Science have become so diffused in forty years as to become a part of the mental property of millions of people who do not know how they got them nor where, but think them instinctively. There are some curious things about this country which people best appreciate who live or travel in other countries. One of them is that the mind of man is freer here than elsewhere. It is less limited and controlled by authority, tradition and instruction here than in Europe. The English mind, which is not so manacled at home but that it has been able to work to some purpose, was still set free on the American continent. We have some awful laws here, and a lot of people with a terrible propensity to make more laws, and some extremely lawless people, but except in time of war, minds in this country are fairly free to work. Our educated people are less trained, shaped, and cultivated than people of their sort in England, but there goes with that deficiency the advantage that there is room left in the American mind for things that are excluded from minds tighter packed. It is an axiom that in spiritual seeking one need expect nothing from the wise. If you get any news it will be from the simple. It accords with that idea that the American mind should be more accessible to spiritual promptings than most minds of Europeans. It

is true that we have in this country by unconscious
inheritance an understanding of some things which
the European mind, as a rule, has never assimilated,
and which it seems to be the aim of current events,
and whatever causes them, to make that mind accept.

I DOUBT that Prohibition is an American idea, and
suspect it of being precisely the contrary, but it
is credited to the United States, and its course here
is watched from near and far.

What have we got out of it and what have we
lost?

The saloons are pretty well closed. The advertisement of intoxicants is dead. The liquor business, manufacture, sales and power of political
corruption is smashed, which might be a good thing
if it were not for the remarkable activity of the
bootlegging business which has succeeded it.

Now what have we lost?

One loss is that there is no longer a fair competition between good drinks and bad. The bad have
an overwhelming advantage. The harder drinks
are more portable and much more easily obtainable.
The good wines are too bulky to be profitably
handled. The quality even of purchasable spirits
has fallen off.

But the worst of the present phase of Prohibition
is that its philosophy is wrong, or at least seems
wrong to a great many perfectly decent and orderly
people. They look upon wine as a legitimate factor
in promoting the joy of life. They do not ask that
it shall be useful, but they insist that it is pleasant,

lawfully pleasant if properly used. They see France and other grape-growing countries running over with good wine, red and white, which they cannot buy lawfully or otherwise. They see their own conviction as to what is right and wrong in drinking subjected by force to the convictions of other people who, they think, are no wiser and no better in morals or character than themselves. They do not like that. They do not like to be forcibly subjected to a righteousness to which they do not subscribe. They think Prohibition laws, as they are, conflict with that measure of liberty of conduct which is necessary to the development of mankind. That is the main objection to Prohibition, the objection that you cannot make men good or wise or even thrifty against their will, and that legislation to accomplish that is worse than useless.

So it is not demonstrated yet that Prohibition is an American idea or one in the operation of which we are more fortunate than other people.

The Bats in Some Belfries

WHAT DO PEOPLE DO WHO HAVE NO BATS IN their belfries? How do they get along at all with minds concerned with nothing more than the prosaic details of life—getting money and spending it, working at their jobs, looking for pleasures or consolations, keeping house, minding children, conducting "drives," giving dinner parties, and such things? Don't they get terribly bored with those exercises? When they need to retire into their thoughts have they any good thoughts to retire into? Have they any likely expectations a little remote from the ordinary to keep in mind, and give them an interest in newspapers and other means of information, to watch for signs that these expectations are making good or the contrary? Life-as-it-is is very cold victual, served up after life-as-it-was has gone by the board, and before life-as-it-to-be has taken form. Books merely about life as it is, which show no consciousness that it is a mere relic of a dead past and no curiosity about where it is driving to, must be food for minds which are very easily satisfied.

Now a good bat or two in one's belfry insures one from being bored to death with worn-out commonplaces. To have lively expectations about the next phase of life and curiosity about any information that purports to throw light on it, is an excellent bat. So everything which is concerned with the extraordinary new developments of the powers of man, whether natural and material or supernatural and elusive, helps to keep the faculties alert and observant. Reasonably good theories about the future of the human race and even about its remote past; exhumed information that throws light on how much human beings had come to know in prehistoric times; information about the derivation of races as we know them, and their probable destiny —all these things are helpful to spirits worn with waiting on the machinations of politicians and the sluggishness of popular majorities. Spiritism is an excellent bat. The theory that the ten lost tribes of Israel are the progenitors to an uncertain extent of races now active in world affairs is a better bat that any normal person who has not examined it could imagine. Everybody who wants to stay really alive had better accept it as true that man is a wonderful creature whose evolution is imperfectly traced, whose limitations are exaggerated, whose powers are almost limitless, about whom what is known is a mere beginning of what is knowable, and that knowledge is still in its infancy, though accumulating at a tremendous rate and reaching out toward marvels which will make our contemporary wonders seem commonplace.

Speculations about the ten lost tribes of Israel and what became of them are not new. One recalls a book published forty years or more ago which argued that the Nestorians, East Syrians of Turkey and Persia, were descended from them. For the last sixty years the lost-articles department of history has been increasingly invaded by inquirers for those tribes. A whole literature about them has grown up, and it is by no means bad reading, and affords information about many curious things, even if it fails of conviction. If the lost tribes perished, then a great deal of space in the Bible has been wasted on their beginning and early history as a part of the Kingdom of Israel. If Jacob's prophetic estimate of his children's qualities is to go for naught, why has it been offered and continued to be offered to millions on millions of Bible readers? Few things in the Old Testament are read as much and have excited as much reflection as those forecasts. It is told in the Bible how the Israelites misbehaved, neglected orders, flirted with idolaters, and "cut up" under the influence of bad associates and weak kings, and how the Kingdom of Israel split and the ten tribes drifted away from the rest, while the tribes of Judah and Benjamin kept on for a while longer as an organized kingdom. At that time the lost tribes pretty well disappeared from the record of history, but that they continued to exist and to cut a figure in the world was confidently believed for many centuries, so that two epistles in the New Testament are addressed to the dispersed part of Israel.

The story of the imaginative people who want to connect the lost tribes with the history of Europe and especially the British Isles, and through them with the American people, begins with an alleged migration of the Prophet Jeremiah to Ireland in the

year B.C. 721. They say he took with him two
royal princesses who were his granddaughters; that
he settled at Tara, which became a center of civilization and presently the seat of a university. Presum-
ably the harp that hung in Tara's halls is the
familiar harp on the Irish flag. That was not all
by a good deal. Other tribes are traced by these
ingenious inquirers to England, partly out of Bible
statements and prophecies, partly by existing monuments, partly by allusions in the writings of profane
historians. The names of nations and tribes, sustaining various changes, are used to trace the movement of the tribes that bore them. So the Saxons
are said originally to have been Isaac's sons and
"British" is alleged to be a word made up from
"Brith," covenant, and "ish," man, and means man
of the Covenant. There is a story that when the
Prophet Jeremiah came to Ireland he brought with
him the stone which is now the seat of the corona-
tion chair of England, which is kept in Westminster
Abbey and in which every English monarch sits
when he is crowned. There is such a chair. There
is such a stone, and it is probably known that it
came from Ireland. Whether the Prophet Jeremiah
brought it there, and whether it is the stone that
Jacob's head rested on when he had his dream and
when he wrestled with the Angel, are matters proper
for discussion and are amply discussed in the various books which relate to the Anglo-Israel suggestion.

The Anglo-Israel people are pretty liberal about
the disposition of the world. They do not insist

that it is all going to the Chosen People, but they are quite strong for the opinion that the tribes of Israel have been nursed along for offices of special usefulness to mankind. They include the Normans and doubtless the Bretons among the peoples who have had an infusion of the prophetic stock. They include the Celts generally, especially the Welsh. One gathers something out of their books about the early intercourse between the countries east of the Mediterranean and the British Isles which is news to most casual readers of history. The upshot of all these curious investigations is that it belongs to the British, the Americans, and the Jews to hang together and work together as descendants of Israel, however mixed with other elements, and that they have in common distinctive purposes which differentiate them from the Latin Nations, and the other peoples of Europe.

Anybody that really wants to qualify as a son of Israel ought to be able to do it. The terms are liberal: the stock is extensively diffused and mixed with other stocks, but watered stock will do. The main inheritance is spiritual, and that may come by assimilation, so the Gentiles may get it.

The suggestion is useful to take some of the curse off of the researches and expositions of Lothrop Stoddard, Charles W. Gould, and Madison Grant, who insist with so much fervor that we must be Nordics or perish. Maybe the Lost Tribes are the real Nordics, or found them sympathetic and grafted on to them. Perhaps some of the tribes of Israel merged into the Teutonic race, which Hou-

ston Chamberlain insisted was the world's white
hope. To be sure, the Nordics were blonds, and
one would expect the Lost Tribes to be dark, but
climate might account for that, and there are light-
haired, and even red-haired, Jews.

A great merit of the Anglo-Israel hypothesis is
that it takes the Jews in out of the cold, and pro-
vides them with blood relatives in a good position
in life. If the British are descendants of Jacob,
even in a diluted degree, the Jews can't complain
because Jerusalem is in British hands. It is still
in the family.

The two great questions that are interesting to us
human creatures are: where did we come from and
where are we going to? Both of them seem in
these times to be in rapid process of elucidation. A
lot is turning up all the time about the world that
was, and a lot more about the world that is to come.
Between the excavations in Egypt, Chaldea, Crete,
Yucatan and other places which reek with antiquity,
and the adventures of the spiritists which constantly
increase in interest and credibility, we seem to be in
good way to get enough information about human
life to live it more successfully than it has been
lived heretofore. Knowledge is not worth anything,
or at least cannot achieve very much, until the
human mind is ready to receive it. Knowledge that
comes before it can be generally understood is very
apt to perish, or at least to lie idle and helpless until
general information, or what we call science, begins
to catch up with it. There is that old diary of Friar
Bacon which seems to have wonderful things in it,

but in his day it was not safe to disclose them, let alone try to make them work. All the way down recorded history, which is a mighty short path considering how old the world is, one finds heads bobbing up that had something in them quite out of the ordinary. The habit was to cut them off if they were troublesome and threatened to interfere too much with the existing order. That is not done now. The custodians of knowledge are very jealous, but they do not kill and burn as much as they did, and science really begins to have some imagination. What has been ascertained is so extraordinary that it helps the case of folks who claim that they have greater wonders still to show. The inferior scientists hold on to the idea that what they don't know is not knowledge, but the top scientists know better. They know that they have only scratched the surface of human life and the purpose of whoever ordained it.

These are anxious times in this world. They worry a great many people, and there is abundant reason for all of their anxieties. The great problems left by the War are working out, of course, but they seem to lag about it. Of Europe, as a whole, there is no existing management that can handle its problems. In so far as they work out, they work out by the action of underlying forces. The great powers try to take care of their own. The League of Nations is able to do something sometimes, but in the main, the great disease of Europe is progressing under the observation of doctors who have no remedies powerful enough to control it.

With Europe in that state, is it surprising that so many people are on the lookout for new developments in man, new knowledge to guide him, new powers to fetch him out of the predicament that he is in? Those are the people who have bats in their belfries. They want to know. They want to understand. They want to see the path cleared to something. They search the Scriptures to an extraordinary extent, compare with what they find there any outside spiritual information which they can pick up, and keep their eyes and ears open to new suggestions. They think that what the world most needs is a better and fuller understanding of human life, and they are far readier than they were five or six years ago to examine anything that promises to be helpful to that understanding. A great many people believe in immortality, believe that the dead go on living and wonder that they have not more to say to us—wonder that out of their enlarged experience they do not make to us more suggestions about the conduct of life. More people all the time entertain the belief that they do make such suggestions, are making them now and are trying systematically to perfect communication with the living.

If the common knowledge of mankind is up to the job of straightening out the complications of this present world, well and good; let the possessors of that knowledge do it. The field is open to them and no one is hindering their efforts. But if the job is too much for them, the possessors of uncommon knowledge may very properly bring to notice whatever they know or think they know that has a bearing on the general situation.

Theological Discussions

THE MAY MEETINGS OF THE PARLIAMENTARY bodies of the Protestant Churches were full of discussion and contention about statements of belief. Methodists, Presbyterians and Baptists all had a turn at it, and were voluminously reported in the newspapers. Mr. Bryan was active in the Presbyterian Assembly, and where Mr. Bryan launches argument and takes definite positions there is usually abundant publicity. There was in this case. Mr. Bryan is opposed, as we all know, to Darwinism or what he thinks is Darwinism, and he fought it in the General Assembly, and tried to get it prohibited from Presbyterian schools, colleges and general thought. He did not quite succeed in that, though he did put through a resolution pledging officers and members of the Presbyterian Church to total abstinence, which was not particularly dangerous because the Presbyterians will doubtless do as they like about taking such a pledge.

The public interest in all these religious controversies has been very lively, and they have been the topic of endless editorial remarks in the newspapers. What has interested the papers and the public has been not so much whether various statements of belief were true or not, as how far the councils of the churches would try to bind their ministers to these beliefs. In both the Presbyterian and Baptist meetings the main row was over orthodoxy. In the Presbyterian meetings Mr. Bryan was beaten as candidate for Moderator, and was not allowed to have his way about evolution, but he did succeed in inducing the Assembly to instruct the Presbytery of New York as to what are essential beliefs, and to command it to instruct its preachers to preach those beliefs. That was particularly a detail of discipline for Dr. Harry Emerson Fosdick, a Baptist who is preaching in a New York Presbyterian church, and being one of the most useful, interesting and religious preachers in town, is very highly regarded by some of his brethren of the pulpit.

The Baptists made a better showing. It seems the Baptist Church does not hold its members to agreement with any creed, which in these times is a very helpful relief. Baptists have opinions as to what is true and what is not, and the councils of the Church doubtless pass on those opinions, and there is no general complaint that the Baptists are not orthodox, but they have this valuable escape from creedal obligations, and nowadays they seem to be happy in it. When the Reverend Straton, an ardent fundamentalist of New York, tried to shut off President Faunce, of Brown University, from addressing the Baptist meeting, Doctor Straton was sat upon promptly and with emphasis by the brethren, and Doctor Faunce made his address.

Members of the Presbytery in New York and others to the number of sixty-six protested against the action which Mr. Bryan was able to induce the General Assembly to take, calling upon the New York Presbytery to require every preacher in Presbyterian pulpits to adhere to the Westminster confession of faith, and in addition to certain specified doctrines, to wit: That there are no errors in the Bible; the Virgin birth of Christ; that He rose from the dead in the same body in which He lived; that by His death he "satisfied Divine justice," and that His miracles were miracles as reported. The sixty-six protested that these beliefs were not essential to belief in Christianity, and that the requirements to entertain them had been added unwarrantably to the requirements of the Presbyterian Church. That does not necessarily imply disbelief on the part of the remonstrants in the propositions mentioned. They went no farther than to say that they were not essential beliefs. This Bryanite resolution was aimed at Doctor Fosdick, but the Baptists, whose fold he belongs in, in their meeting refused all invitations to meddle with him.

A categorical reply to the resolution of the Assembly was made in the newspapers by Dr. Henry S. Coffin of New York, one of the sixty-six, and a notable Presbyterian preacher. He denied that any of the five propositions was an essential doctrine in the form in which the Assembly's resolution stated it, and said he did not personally accept and teach any of them in that form. He did not believe the Scriptures claim to be "without error," nor find that they proclaimed the Virgin birth as an essential doctrine; he would not accept "satisfied

Divine justice" as a competent disclosure of what Christ's death accomplished, nor agree that the Scriptures teach that Christ rose from death in the same body in which He lived, nor that Christ considered faith in His miracles essential. Yet in his comments Doctor Coffin gave evidence of being appreciably Christianized, even though not in agreement with all particulars of doctrine as stated under the compelling inspiration of Mr. Bryan. He said that if Doctor Fosdick wasn't fit to preach in a Presbyterian pulpit neither was he, for he shared Fosdick's point of view.

Awful, they seem, these disagreements of doctors, but in reality they are not so bad. They will all be reconciled in time if the human mind is allowed to work. Mr. Bryan seems to want to chain it up, and that's where Mr. Bryan is wrong. In religion, as in prohibition, he believes in compulsion, and in that he is crudely antagonistic to the Christian philosophy; but in his doctrinal beliefs he is not far out, though his statement of them should not be imposed upon anybody. No one should be tied up to the assertion that the Bible is without error. To do that is simply to use that remarkable collection of books as a slung-shot to crack heads with. The Bible is by far the most valuable depository of human experience that exists. There is more truth about religion in it than in all the rest of the library. To dig out that truth and digest it is a big job, but it better repays labor than any other form of excavation now being prosecuted. The Bible tells what sort of creatures men are, how they came so, how they have behaved in times past, and how their Maker has dealt with them. It offers the best available clues to proper behavior, and the best suggestions to be had for keeping this world and its inhabitants from going once more to the demnition bowwows. It contains such extraordinary deposits of truth, recognizable as truth by competent minds, that the notion that it is miraculously errorless is excusable. But to think it errorless is not only not a duty, but is a hindrance to progress in understanding it. Search the Scriptures by all means, but search it for errors as well as for information.

The Bible is full of marvels, indicating potentialities in men that are still incompletely developed and understood. It is full of the suggestion of an invisible world closely associated with this material world and into which we graduate when we have finished with life here, and with which we are encouraged to have such dealings as we can while we are still clothed in mortality. It gives no encouragement to all people to think alike, but on the contrary supports a great variety of opinions. It is a book of as much confusion to. the timid or the strait-laced as it is to the wicked; a wonderful, old, middle-of-the-road book, that tramps down the main street of history, turning out for no one, indifferent to kings, politicians and priests, unchanged in any material degree and unabated as we have it for fifteen hundred years anyhow, and scholars know how much longer. How can one fail to admire the gameness of that old book, usually in the thick of controversy,

flouted, denied, called out-of-date, burned at the
stake, misquoted to the purposes of the Ad-
versary, the inspiration of innovators, the refuge
of cranks, but still somehow always holding its
own between its venerable covers, and waiting,
generation after generation, century after century,
for the world to catch up with it? The doctors of
one generation say: "The Bible truly set forth the
understanding men had of things in its day, but
we know better now." But the wise men of the next
generation are likely to find that the rapid accumu-
lation of knowledge and experience in even a third
of a century has made the Bible assertions which
their fathers doubted become credible.

Consider miracles. Doctor Coffin does not think
belief in the miracles of Christ is an essential doctrine, and perhaps it is not, but the current of everyday experience in these times strongly favors the
fact that Christ did miracles in healing. The belief
grows all the time not only that extraordinary cures
were done by Christ, but that they were a part of
His teaching, and can still be done and are being
done every day in many places by many people.
For anyone who is curious on that subject, the
writer of an article in *The Ladies' Home Journal*
for June has gathered a good deal of interesting information. "Are There Modern Miracles?" is the
title of the article, and the author tells about alleged
cures of an extraordinary nature made mostly by
healers connected with various churches, and believed in and encouraged by churchmen as eminent

as Bishop Manning and Bishop Brent, and many
others.

The way to find out whether the New-Testament
stories about miracles are true is to look around and
see what is going on now. The New-Testament
stories cannot well be verified, but these current
tales can be run down, and there are very many of
them. Some of the doctors take careful notice of
them, trying to verify statements concerning them,
and where they think the statements are true, try to
discover and understand by what force the cures are
accomplished. The Rockefeller Foundation is one
powerful and scientific body that is interested to
add to knowledge in this field. It urges a study of
healing by suggestion, a branch of the curative art
which, in its opinion, modern medicine has
neglected. The Christian Scientists have worked
this branch diligently, and one notices that their
church is growing fast, and according to latest re-
ports is very active and prosperous, so that though
Doctor Coffin may not think belief in miracles a
doctrine essential to Presbyterians, he must realize
that the failure to believe in them in some form
may involve a loss of spiritual power.

When he says that he does not consider the
Virgin birth an essential doctrine he seems to be
right. "Personally," he says, "I do not know how
our Lord was born," but if so, he seems to be in no
worse condition that St. Paul or most of the
Apostles. The story of the Virgin birth in the New
Testament is in very good company indeed, being
included in a narrative of occurrences which are a

part of the essence of the Christian religion. While the story of the Virgin birth cannot be proved, it may seem probable or improbable according as it is supported or not by new knowledge concerning the whole mystery of creation.

In the matter of the resurrection of Christ and what kind of body He rose in, there may be help had from the experience of the spiritists from Swedenborg down, and including many investigators now active, who seem to have good information and quite clear ideas about the nature and composition of that part of us which is immortal. President Vincent, of the Rockefeller Foundation, says of modern medicine that "it seeks to be open-minded toward new truth, provided this can be rationally related to the great body of firmly established and organized knowledge about nature, life, and mind, about which all scientific men agree." The same thing should be true of modern religion. It should be open-minded toward new truth provided it can be rationally related to the truth of the statements in the Bible about which all Christians must agree. For the Bible, to Christians, is the great test of new truth, the touchstone which determines whether or not it is wholesome, whether or not it is trustworthy. But the judges nowadays are not much the General Assemblies and church parliaments, but the individual readers, who finding things happen which they don't understand, come to the Bible as inquirers, to get light on these novelties. Just as the trust of the peoples of the world in their govern-

ments is impaired, so is the confidence of the religious people in the opinions of their church authorities.   The world is full of seekers, both in politics
and in religion.   They feel an immense need of
something better than they have had, something
with more power to help in it.   In the churches
as in government, power is passing from the hands
of men whose minds and opinions were formed before 1914, and into the hands of men whose most
impressive teacher was the Great War, and who
want a world in which recurrence of wholesale
calamity like that will be impossible.   Seeing that
pre-war governments and economics and the rise of
industrialism could not safeguard human life, they
want something that can.   Seeing that pre-war
Christianity lacked the power to conserve society,
they want a Christianity or a something else that
will have that power and use it.   Feeling so, they
are bad partisans in politics and worse, if anything, in religion, but are attentive to events, and
while they will not aimlessly detach themselves
from the organizations they are used to work with,
they keep looking out for something to make them
more helpful.

That is a fit temper for great adventures in
thought and government.   The old hands in charge
watch it with more or less dismay, and try to guide
it, but it seems to be developing a will very much
its own, a scattered will at present, uncertain what
to back, but capable, under fit leadership, of union
and great accomplishment.   Doctor Marquis says

of Henry Ford. "He has the not uncommon conviction that he has a real message for the world, a
real service to render mankind. He has in him the
makings of a great man if only the parts of him,
lying about in more or less disorder, were properly
assembled." So it is with the generation that has
come since the War and is waiting to take charge of
human life. It has great parts not yet assembled,
great powers, great impulses, a great vision, but is
not yet hitched up to anything definite. It reads
the newspapers and watches the disputes of politicians and doctors of divinity. Probably it does
not search the Scriptures very zealously, but it can't
fail to notice how great a factor the Bible still is in
human affairs.

Stevenson is not too much of an ancient to be
appreciated by the younger generation, and Stevenson being a Scotsman came to be a very diligent
Bible reader. The narrative of Mr. Whitmee of
his association with Stevenson in Samoa has a great
deal about Stevenson as a Bible reader, for Mr.
Whitmee is a minister and Stevenson's religious
propensities interested him. He said Stevenson had
no doubt of the divine inspiration of the Bible, and
he quotes him as wondering that "you preachers,"
as he said, "do not study more teachings of the
prophets, for in my belief they supply the key to the
future of the world." Stevenson thought that
preachers generally took all the real punch out of
the prophets by spiritualizing their utterances and
making them seem to apply to the church, which

was not at all what the writers really had in mind. The prophetic books, he said, were full of teachings which taken literally would be inspiring and a magnificent assurance of a glorious future, but as applied to the church are a comedy.

Prohibition: Advertisement: Organization

OME REMARKS ABOUT PROHIBITION HAVE given dissatisfaction to a lady in Minnesota. She writes about it at some length, expressing especial displeasure with a quotation from Towner's *Philosophy of Civilization* which sets forth that the drinking nations have always beaten the non-drinking nations in all particulars worth mentioning. That is Mr. Towner's assertion and not the assertion of this writer, but, roughly speaking, it seems true. Drink and civilization have usually come along hand-in-hand. Peoples not capable of making and handling intoxicants have not been capable of progressive civilization. In visible things, the drinking nations have got pretty well to the front, though whether it was because they had alcohol, or in spite of it, is not so clear.

Mr. Towner's argument about it is worth attention from persons who have never thought of alcohol as anything but a poison, a noxious thing to be exterminated. Mr. Brisbane said the other day that it would be sixty years before we knew whether Prohibition did good or harm. He thought it would take a couple of generations at least to test the effects of it. The people who think it a great panacea, do not realize in what degree they are betting on an uncertainty. It is a gamble. If it really prevails and lasts, it may do us good, it may do us damage, but no one can estimate the net result.

"It is now an accepted fact," writes our friend in Minnesota, "that those who use alcohol habitually as a beverage, even moderately, are far less immune to disease than those who abstain entirely from its use. That alcohol is one of the most pronounced obstructions to sound judgment and pure thought is accepted by scientists, and is evinced by the fact that business firms everywhere prefer to employ men who do not use alcohol as a beverage and many firms refuse to employ any but total abstainers from its use." "Now in the face of these truths," she says, "what is there to say?"

It may be said, for one thing, that accepted facts must be judged by the qualifications of the persons who accept them. For many centuries it was an accepted fact that the sun moved and the earth stood still, and anyone who denied it was likely to get into trouble with the authorities. The lady in Minnesota is advised not to lean too heavily on the accepted facts of the apostles of Prohibition, nor even of the unidentified authorities whom she calls "the scientists," but to rely as much as possible on her own observations. If she sees people who she knows are not rigid abstainers, getting along with life, useful and respected, and as healthy as other people, she may suspect that not all the information she has accepted is sound. If, as is possible, the opportunity to observe drinking except in its more objectionable forms is no longer good—and possibly never has been good—in her town, perhaps she will take the word of another observer that hereabouts, before Prohibition, total abstainers were few, yet things went along pretty well, and work was done, bills paid, families raised, churches supported, and a large proportion of the children went to school. Moreover, this observer read in the newspaper two days ago, and accepted it as probably true, that in the course of the last hundred years, while the demon Rum was ramping and roaring up and down these now regenerated States, and obstructing the intellects and facilitating the diseases of his victims, the expectation of life increased by fifteen years.

The function of alcohol is not to promote sound judgment and pure thought. It is not often good at that. Work and drink go better apart. The main use of drink is for relaxation, though for some people it works in usefully as a detail of diet. Wisely used it makes dinner parties livelier, public dinners more tolerable, wedding guests more blithe and life in general pleasanter.

Has the lady in Minnesota happened lately to dip into *The Pilgrim's Progress?* The observer, feeling the need of pious guidance, did so the other day and was astonished and a little appalled at the circulation of rum through that holy volume. The pilgrims were constantly having drinks poked at them to put distance between themselves and the City of Destruction. Not the ungodly gave them reviving draughts, and cordials, and flasks to carry with them in case of emergency, but the demure and saintly entertainers whose office it was to give the pilgrims rest and lodging and send them on their way.

Avoid that book, dear lady in Minnesota. It is sadly out of date. The Bible is by no means up to the level of the Eighteenth Amendment, but it doesn't reek with rum as Bunyan does.

Rum is dangerous, but so are lots of other things —poison gas, airplanes, divorce, delay, the new explosives that await the next war, the creeds, the preachers, the Senate, spiritism, nationalism, internationalism, legislation, half-knowledge. Almost everything that has any punch in it is dangerous. Are we to abolish all such things, or is it better to get along with them? There is no good gift that some folks will not abuse. From birth to death we go our pilgrimage with our lives in our hands, but who wouldn't rather carry them so than entrust them to the care of a committee! If Prohibition is an attempt to buy physical well being at cost of spiritual welfare it will do harm. Courage and self-control are spiritual qualities. Can we spare them? Prohibition is confession that we cannot manage rum. But we ought to. To some extent it is good, and we ought to have that good, and if we have the right stuff in us we can profit by it. But Prohibition says we are beaten and must give up our birthright.

It is honestly doubted by thousands of decent, intelligent, and well-informed persons whether the abolition of alcohol as a beverage is to be desired. The reasons for this doubt are not hard to come by.

Those who entertain it do not entertain it because they are devoted to rum. As compared with the public welfare in the long run, the pleasures of drink do not weigh with them much. They think the cost of Prohibition is too great, morally, physically, and financially. They think the final result of it will not be good, but bad. They think the drink problem can be, and ought to be so handled that the maximum of good will result and a minimum of mischief. What the Minnesota lady and thousands of others of her sort should really try to understand is that there is another side to the drink question.

But really there is no need to worry or make long arguments about Prohibition. People are getting philosophical about it. It is going to take care of itself. Where the Solons and the Dracos who have devised its provisions have fallen short, the common citizens on whom it falls to apply them will bring the necessary remedies. Where the restrictions meet with due measure of approval they will stand; where they turn out to do more harm than good and make more trouble than they are worth, they will fall into disuse. If the Amendment lasts long enough it will probably develop domestic wine-making and perhaps domestic brewing on an extensive scale. The real enemy that the Prohibition law was made to fight was the merchandising of intoxicants, the crowding of them on the market, the cultivation of a demand for them by too much advertising and too many saloons. What brought on Prohibition was the highly developed

salesmanship of the distillers, the liquor dealers
and brewers.

What will salesmanship do next? It is a very
modern thing in the degree in which we now have it.
Advertisement is its brother and sister, and that also
in its present development is novel and unmeasured.
What a din is made in this modern world by folks
who want to sell things! What an extraordinary
place they have made for themselves! They are
the foundation on which stands the whole contemporary structure of newspapers and periodicals.
This dependence of the press upon the advertiser is
one of a lot of processes that are working out almost
imperceptibly. The results come along so gradually
and with so little noise that when they arrive one
starts back at the sight of them notwithstanding he
has been looking on at their advance since they
were in the cradle. One remembers if he is old
enough, when there were still dry-goods stores, but
now there are department stores with dry goods as
one detail in them. There goes on a constant
organization of everything—the swallowing up of
small fish by great. The system of branch banks
is just now struggling for country-wide extension.
There is opposition and maybe it won't spread beyond local limits, but the chain stores are going
everywhere—cigar stores, more recently groceries,
milk stores, fruit stores and who knows what not?
These innovations ought to bring the consumer
nearer to the maker and the grower. They do,
probably, when they begin and until the opposition

of the individual concerns is killed off.   What happens then ought to be disclosed by statistics on the cost of living.

If someone would expound the limits of organization that would be helpful.   If all the visible world is to be organized, access to the invisible world must be improved for the relief of folks who want to go their own gait.   If life is to be impossible in this world except on the herd basis, not everyone will like the prospect.   We must think out, somehow, how much of us it is necessary to organize, and how much can escape.

Moreover, the nations must do the same.   The League of Nations is an organization to escape war. The alternative to it—armament—preparedness— also implies organization.   One may prefer the League because it involves less organization than the other way; also because it may do the job and we know by long experience that preparedness won't.

Organization nowadays seems indispensable to accomplish any considerable thing in human affairs, but still at the heart of it all is individualism, and without that it can get nowhere.   So there is something about us that can be organized, and something that is and always must be individual and which we must never suffer to merge with the herd if we are to amount to anything.   The League of Nations is a plan to save the world by organization, but Mr. Wilson, its chief designer and promoter, was as distinct an individualist as one could find.

At this writing his funeral is just over, and his character and political career have been the main topics of public discussion for five days, crowding into second place even the apprehensive considerations of the oil scandals in Washington. The end of that discussion is nowhere in sight, though, of course, it will subside enough to give room to thought and speech about current matters that require settlement. It is likely to run more or less through this 'year's presidential campaign, and possibly will determine what issues shall govern it.

Mr. Wilson had come to be the most interesting human figure in the world; probably the most noted man; possibly the most revered. We are very apt to see men bigger than they really are at the moment of their death. The concentration of thought on them that is induced by their departure usually exaggerates them. And so perhaps current feeling about Mr. Wilson is exaggerated; but we cannot tell about that until the final results of his labors have worked out and it is possible to estimate what he accomplished. He was President of the United States at the time of a great crisis in human affairs in which the United States finally played a great part. It is great crises that make great men, but only provided that characters show up that are capable of great development. You can beat iron into a sword, but there must be iron to beat. Beat you ever so skilfully you cannot make a sword out of a lath.

There was iron in Mr. Wilson, and it stood a lot of beating before it broke. There are many who see

in him the greatest, most potent and most useful
character of his time. Their belief in him is very
deep. What will justify it, if it is justified, is the
final triumph of that conception of the co-operation
of the nations to prevent war with which his name
is identified, and to the furtherance of which he gave
all he had.

The Rattle of Machinery

RE THERE TOO MANY PEOPLE IN THE world?

There are those who think so and who knowing the very rapid increase in the world's population, affect to tremble at the prospect of subsistence growing barer and barer and the competition for it constantly increasing in intensity.

They make out a case that is impressive, if one accepts their facts. They think mankind nowadays is living improvidently, wasting the accumulations of ages, and expanding in numbers like pioneers in a new country. But they hold that pioneering is over for this world, that there are virtually no more new lands to be brought under civilization, and that the supply of food can be increased only by intensive agriculture.

There is something in all that; not so much, probably, as its propounders believe, but enough to think about and inquire about, and as an argument for small families it is commended to the attention of people who think the limitation of progeny is the indispensable preliminary to better times on earth. But what has it all to do with the desire of the postmen for an increase of pay? They want one. They have this aspiration now and then, and, being general favorites, their desires usually receive hospitable attention and go to Congress highly

recommended. They are overworked and under-
paid—so they say, and it is probably true. Very
well.

The amount of matter going through the mails
has enormously increased in recent years. What
has increased it? Are there more lovers who write
daily to beloved objects? Are the absent sons more
filial in communicating with their parents? Is there
a greater correspondence between friends? Oh, yes.
Probably there is some increase in all of these
particulars. But it is just a normal increase. This
huge mass of letter mail that swells the postal
revenues, but still more the work of the postmen, is
not due to the increase of normal correspondence.
It is due to the immense use of the post office as a
cheap means of advertising. We all know that.
Nobody has to assure us of what we have ample
evidence every morning in the mail and every time
the postman stops in the course of the day. Neither
do we need anyone to tell us that this vast encroach-
ment of mail advertisements on breakfast and the
other incidents of domestic life is a part of the
urgency of competition for the means of subsistence
which has come from the increased population and
the extraordinary and somewhat ominous development of the means of communication between the
human beings now on earth. If there continue to
be more and more people, and more and more need
of selling things, and more and more advertisements
in the mail, and more and more uninvited solicitations for our attention, how long will it be before
we shall be quite swept off our legs by the ava-

lanches of mail matter and the other related
assaults?   Noah got word that there was a flood
coming and built an ark to save his family and
samples of the animals.   What kind of an ark
shall we build to save us from the too great pressure
of invitations to buy upon our limited powers of
attention and means of purchase?

Human life has changed so much even in twenty
years that old practices and methods are constantly
taking on new energy and running away with us.
It is like the rabbits in Australia.   They were taken
there and, because no conveniences for restricting
them had even been developed, they ran away from
all control, multiplied enormously and became a
nuisance.   That sort of thing is happening to us
all the time.   Consider the automobiles in the cities.
They are an innovation.   The right way to handle
them has not been fully worked out yet, and so
everywhere they show more or less propensity to
crowd human life off the map.   They keep legis-
lators, traffic cops, and constables on the jump to
contrive to keep them in their place.   They are indispensable.   Nobody wants to abolish them, but
nearly everyone has to give some thought to the
proper limitation of their activities and pervasive-
ness.   Advertising is much the same.   Nobody wants
to abolish that, but neither do folks in general
desire that the post office should exist mainly as a
convenience for advertisement and only secondarily
for the benefit of folks who have nothing to sell but

something to communicate one to another. The propensity of advertisement in these times is to crowd in as the most important thing of life and the thing without which the rest of life can no longer get along. In the periodicals it has pretty well accomplished that aspiration, and it is making pretty good in the mails. It uses every new discovery, every novel application of knowledge. It fills the streets at night with electric signs. One reads that it is working into radio, and that rates are being made for the intrusion of solicitations to buy in the news and the noises that go about by wireless.

Some of us may recall the scandal that arose when the Interborough Company in New York rented out the walls of its stations to advertising men. The stations had been lined with tiles and were handsome, with pretty decorations in colors bordering them. The public sense was shocked at their disfigurement. It did not matter, the disfigurement was promptly accomplished and has stayed accomplished in the line first built, only more so, ever since, so that it is difficult to discover the name of a station in the garish setting that crowds round it, but the new subways were defended from this perversion by a prohibition when they were built, and that is encouraging. So the wayside advertising. Everybody knows about that. There is a constant fight against it, and some day the fight will win. It is winning now in some states, but the point is that advertisement in all its forms is an enormous force carefully designed to affect the will of the people, to excite their desires, to direct their expenditure—a very powerful force profoundly selfish, going loose in the world without any restraint except its ability to pay and an obligation not to offend the simpler forms of the moral sense of the public. As mankind grows wiser, if indeed it does grow wiser, we may see advertisement regulated, as the sale of drink or of narcotics is regulated, or possibly prohibited altogether, unless indeed a different policy comes to pass in time, and drink and everything else is let loose and people are invited to take care of themselves.

There is a connection between the power of advertising and of the revenues that are derived from it and the current propensity of newspapers and periodicals to be concentrated in the control of strong hands. When the papers, whose main purpose is the circulation of ideas and the advocacy of social or political policies, come into competition with the papers whose chief concern is the diffusion of goods and the acquirement of the resulting revenues, the papers which deal in ideas are apt to go to the wall. The others are too strong for them. They can buy away both their contributors and their supporters. They can vastly out-advertise them.

But all these are temporary conditions. Advertisement is in the condition of the rabbit in Australia before the Australians woke up to appreciation of what was going on, and so is the linking up up newspapers and the cutting of the throats of those whose existence is not so profitable to some buyer as that of other papers whose ideas suit him better and whose prosperity he wishes to promote.

After all, this world as it is is a grand "catch-as-catch-can" world, proceeding rapidly through space, revolving at a fair gait on its own axis, and humming considerably on its surface as above remarked. Who is for slowing it up? This matter of advertisement is just a detail of its current speed, and there is plenty to be said for that speed. If it were shut off and some second-speed provided for us that would be easier on our machinery, probably we should not like it. "England, with all thy faults I love thee still," said Cowper, that melancholy poet, one hundred and forty years ago, and that is a proper sentiment to have about this world now, if one thinks that with all its clamors and all its blares and glares it is really getting somewhere. There is a basis for that opinion. The great preliminary to progress is to get out of ruts. If there ever was a time when this world got out of more ruts in twenty-five years than it has done since the beginning of the century, when was that time? Whole sets of conceptions of life have gone by the board. Religion has changed. The conception of the woman's job in the world has changed. The old-time notions of the usefulness of kings and of what sort of men should govern nations have changed enormously. The activities of people who seem to have the improvement of human life on their minds are extraordinary. The rising generation will undertake anything, especially the girls in it. The real chance for Prohibition is in the idea that this generation of men in this country is so stimulated spiritually and mentally that they do not need rum any more.

Shall Business Run the World?

O YOU THINK THIS WOULD BE A BETTER world if people spoke their minds more freely? Or do you think the main effect would be increased expenditure for police?

There is a good deal of complaint that speech is not free enough, especially in the newspapers and periodicals. Those institutions, one hears, discuss only safe topics and those in a manner acceptable to Business; they do not like to say anything or suggest anything that is not acceptable to Business: that is because their primary concern is not a diffusion of truth but the infusion of money. You must not blame them for that. If they do not make money they cannot live, and if they are not alive they cannot say anything. So, reticence on unprofitable subjects is just a natural condition—the same sort of condition which makes a clam open or shut its shell according to the state of the tide.

Doctor Jacks of Oxford observed in the December *Atlantic* that "religion is being presented to the world to-day in forms which are quite inadequate to the problem it has to solve." Which is probably true. Would it not be profitable then to get up a great discussion about the forms in which religion is being presented and whether they are adequate, and if not, what forms would be adequate? Perhaps so. But when a publisher of various periodicals was asked the other day, "Won't you please get up a big discussion in your magazine as to whether there is more of the spirit of Christianity in the Catholic Church, the Methodist Church, Harvard College, the Standard Oil Company, or the Steel Trust," what did he say? He said, "Excuse me, if you please! The last time I started a discussion on religion in our magazine it cost me three hundred thousand dollars."

All the same, the discussion proposed would be interesting if the participants were able enough, and if any of them had a true notion of what the spirit of Christianity really is. And these five powerful corporations just named—have they all got some of it? No doubt they have, all of them. You may agree with Doctor Jacks as above that religion is not being shot into us to-day out of the right kind of machine guns, or you may agree with Mary Austin in the December *Century* that the real mind of Christ is not taught in the churches; but when one comes to think about it he must realize that even the most secular of those corporations named has touched the hem of Christ's garment and felt the virtue that comes out of him. They are all in some measure Christianized. So in our time is industry in general, and science and education are going to be when they get round to it, and one has good hope even for the ecclesiastical corporations. They cannot escape the spirit of which there is so much in the world and more coming.

How much good would more discussion do us? You observe who it is that always calls for more discussion—more talk about everything? It is the talkers. They are good at talk and it seems to them that free discourse will save the world. No doubt in a democracy there is great virtue and value in the courageous discussion of public affairs. When it seems bad for business we may not get enough of it, but still it always goes on by word of mouth between man and man and in small companies. In the late election public discussion seemed to do almost nothing. What the newspapers printed seemed to have no great effect. The mind of the people seemed to work independently of them all. Some money was spent that may have done something, but not nearly enough to win the election. It was not bought. The public mind reached its conclusion apparently in private, but it reached it.

The newspapers and the other periodicals do better than they get credit for. They lie low, but they bide their time, and when occasion offers they blurt out everything they can get hold of. There are so many of them, and all competing more or less for the news and all new knowledge! They are the very sails of civilization; not indeed the wind that moves it, but the sails that catch the wind. Where else do you go to find out what is in the air? If there is a man who knows a new thing, some newspaper or some periodical tells about him and what he knows. If there is a book that has a valuable idea the reviewers usually impart it to us before we see the book. Admitting that print can become a nuisance, still it is a wonderful thing, and the free competition in the sale of it is very valuable. What the reputable papers and "the quality" among the magazines won't print because their constituents are too fastidious to bear it is meat for the more adventurous publications—the very thing they want. A good many persons are prone to stop their paper or magazine when it hints something which is contrary to their views and disturbs them. But that is the very time to go on. We need to be disturbed. There is more, far more, to learn than we know, and we do not learn anything very important except by processes which disturb what we know already. When the *Freeman*, lately deceased, started publication, some writer in the *Sun* expressed hope for it because he said it made him mad in seven different ways. The hope indeed failed, but it was well grounded. No great improvement in life can be accomplished without infuriating the folks who like life just as it is. But their very fury helps. It is the resistance of the air that makes the airplane rise, the resistance of the water that makes the ship hold her course when the sails fill. Resistance is valuable; but refusal to know, to observe, to consider is not valuable at all. The newspapers do much to save us from that by insisting that we shall take notice of what is going on. We may not like the headlines they use in that service or the sort of news they thrust upon us, but we do take notice.

What is happening in the world just now? Is there a wave of reaction? The election of Mr. Coolidge with so great an emphasis has been gen-

erally interpreted to mean that Business is taking
charge of the country. The defeat of Ramsay
MacDonald in England seems to have very much
the same significance. Authority seems to be
looking up a bit all over the world. Perhaps it is
necessary that it should, but it is a modified authority. Baldwin's new government in England
is a Tory government to be sure, but one with the
die-hards left out of it. It would not be safe to
call it a backward-looking government. It has to
go on where MacDonald left off, and if it is to
stay in power it must not scandalize the Liberals.
Certainly here Mr. Coolidge's government is not
felt to be backward looking. The bitter-enders are
mostly out of it. Mr. Coolidge as an elected President with a big majority back of him is expected to
be more progressive in international matters than
he has been while operating as Mr. Harding's legal
successor. He shows nothing of the temper of the
men who fought Wilson in the Senate. Progress
comes by waves, and the crest of one wave has
gone by and we are wallowing a bit in a trough.
But there is no convincing evidence yet of a relapse
in the direction of the good old way.

The imposition of authority is always a matter
of nice judgment. There must be authority, but
there must also be the largest measure of free will
consistent with order, not always immediate order
but certainly eventual order. More or less organization is necessary to modern industrial life.
A considerable degree of order is necessary to
organization. A considerable degree of free will is

necessary to progress, and unless progress goes on
the great aim both of authority and organization is
defeated.

Mr. Wilson's great fight at Princeton was in
support of the opinion that the college ought not
to be controlled by Business. That same contention is likely to raise its head from time to time
in most of the colleges. The way Business imparts
money to the cause of education in this country is
something astonishing. Its motives are usually
unselfish. Business has money and it has pretty
well discovered that it must do good with it or
suffer. Its favorite way of doing good with it is
to spend it on education, and especially in the
construction of buildings. Education nowadays
has more wants than an opera singer. Business
is very useful to supply the means to provide for
all these wants, but when it has done it the critics,
especially the young ones, are sure to say that it is
working for its own pocket and mainly in the interest of Business. Of course it is working according to its lights, and its lights are not always
identical with truth, but still it is rash to wish to
break Business of its current concern about education. It seems a case where the tares, if they
are tares, had better be left to grow up with the
wheat. And assuredly the confidence of Business
in Knowledge implies a confidence that Business
can stand the light.

When Business gets to running things too much
there is sure to be a reaction and a more or less
violent surge toward something else; for of course,

Business does tend to think itself the whole of life, and of course it is not that. Mr. William Allen White has written a book about Mr. Wilson—a very interesting book, interesting especially as a study in heredity—disclosing the tremendous qualities from the Scotch-Irish stock that were in him, and the very strong religious bent of his mind. Mr. White exhibits him mainly as a Calvinist, a Presbyterian. Now heaven knows what it means to be a Calvinist, but whatever else Calvinism implies it certainly implies determination that material concerns shall not rule or thwart the concerns of the spirit, nor organization dwarf the individual in man. Mr. Wilson had that in him deep down, ineradicable, never to be compromised. Mr. White pays due attention to his faults but applauds the spirit that was in him. It drove him to the accomplishment of many things which are all but universally conceded to be valuable even to Business, and finally brought him to be an impassioned leader in a war against materialism entrenched and defiant. The thing that Mr. White does not tell about Mr. Wilson was how much he got out of the invisible world. According to his Calvinistic lights he was always trying to hitch his wagon to it; always conscious of something else beyond visible facts; always prayerful and addicted to retirement into that Kingdom of God that was within him. He would doubtless have agreed that though there must be material combinations for spirit to work through, nothing can finally save the world but religion—not mere organized mundane religion as such, but spirit; the link between the visible and invisible worlds; something that will affect the wills of men, modify their aspirations, clarify their perceptions of what is really valuable. By mere authority it is not possible to make marriage successful, or check the deterioration in quality that goes with mass production, or put into factory work something that will feed the soul; but by faith all wonders can be done.

How contemptuous of human opinion is Destiny in its selection of leaders in time of crisis! When there are certain necessary things to be done, someone is prodded into the limelight who can do those things. The qualities which qualify him for that service count. The rest of him may be anything. Most people are slow to realize that. In a great leader they want all-round perfection of character and abilities. They almost never get it. They get only such abilities and such character as are necessary to the job.

Now again that question about Business and whether it is to run the world. That is nowadays a real question. Who shall run the world anyhow? The churches? No! The politicians? They are not overgood at it. Science? Science knows something and it is rather more open-minded than the churches; it really is progressive, and it certainly is a factor—and a great one—in the management of the world, but it is by no means to be trusted to tackle the whole job. It still misses too much; is too opinionative, too confident of its own omniscience. Who is running the world as it is? Business more than anything else. Who is really reconstructing Europe? The governments? No, the bankers; and the bankers are Business.

There is no objection to Business managing the world if it is the best force to do it, but it cannot do it successfully except as it is spiritualized. Is it becoming spiritualized? Perhaps it is. Sometimes it seems so. The New York *World* the other day quoted a Hindu philosopher in a discourse about Business, and especially the American business man. He made a distinction between him and the business man of Europe. He spoke of his quick decisions, of his "hunches" not based so much on facts as on intuition. What does it mean, he says, this "hunch," this impulse? And his answer is: "It means that the business man has listened to a voice from within him—that he has hearkened to some mysterious guiding and counseling force that is deeply hidden in his being; it is some spirit that urges him, commands him to act as he does, for the best. It means that he has recognized a 'superhuman' intelligence at work in his own soul."

There may be more truth in that than most people realize. When we talk to-day about Business we are talking about something different than was covered by the same word thirty, or twenty, or even ten years ago. The War was not in vain. The world is becoming spiritualized. Business shows it. Science shows it. Education and the churches are aware of their great need of it. All the great departments of human activity are working nowadays to save the world. If they can be sufficiently spiritualized they can do it. The leadership among them will go where the capacity for that leadership exists and minor faults and imperfections will not hinder it. If Business has that capacity in the greatest degree, let it go to Business. It is no time to be scared by names. But if Business is to manage the world it must be Big Business: very big, indeed—comprehending all things.

A Little Out of Common

 REQUEST HAS COME IN THE MAIL, AND from a lady. "It is only this, that you take the prologue of Maeterlinck's *The Great Secret* as well as his description of the Pyramid of Cheops as a text for a little discourse designed to take down the inordinate conceit of Americans in our present civilization."

It goes on: "I am an American spending the winter in an English colony and I find the English are almost as bad as we are. However, I am only interested in enlightening the Americans, as I am naturally more fond of them, so that we at least may not make ourselves ridiculous in the eyes of the Oriental nations, with whom we are coming in contact more and more, and who are steeped in the ancient traditions. So many Americans actually believe we are not only the greatest but the most enlightened in all the arts and sciences of any nation that *ever* lived!!! When the truth seems to be that compared with ancient Egypt and India in almost everything, we are merely 'babes in the wood'!"

"In almost everything." That leaves room for exceptions and the exceptions seem rather important. So far as we know we have beaten the ancient Egyptians and Hindus in applied mechanics. No Ford car has as yet been brought out of an Egyp-

tian tomb. Possibly our roads are better than
theirs: they are pretty good nowadays. Our
plumbing is quite good and, what is perhaps more
important, the great mass of people in our time—
and for example in this country—are in a more
forward state of intelligence and knowledge than
the great mass of the people of any country have
ever before been in the history of the world, so
far as we know it. What knowledge we get seems
nowadays to have a better chance for distribution
and assimilation by great numbers of people than
it has ever had before.

So it seems to us; but perhaps we vaunt ourselves
unduly, for we do seem to know extremely little
as yet about the ancient world. We do not even
any longer begin to know how far back what
we call civilization goes. Less than a century ago
pious people put the creation of the world about
four thousand years behind us. Probably not even
Mr. Bryan has confidence any longer in that estimate. Everything that turns up, that is dug up,
that is learned by deciphering inscriptions, that is
suggested in any way, plausible or fantastic, puts
civilization farther and farther back, and some
things credit very ancient prehistoric civilizations
with extraordinary knowledge and accomplish-
ments.

This book of Maeterlinck's that our kind correspondent speaks of has to do mainly with old-time
knowledge of the invisible world. In that, Maeterlinck suspects, the old-timers beat us quite out of
sight. In the beginning of the Bible—in the very

first part of Genesis—there are intimations which
seem to support that theory. It is a theory which
helps to explain the theological conception about the
Fall of Man. Maybe Man did get a fall; there
is a good deal to make one think so, but that need
not conflict with the doctrine of evolution because
the evolutionary periods are so very protracted
that if the human race came a tumble a mere
twenty or thirty thousand years ago and got a set-
back, that would have been a mere ripple in evolution. What Maeterlinck is concerned about, as
he says in his Prologue, is "to discover the source,
to ascend the course and unravel the underground
network of that great mysterious river which since
the beginning of history has been flowing beneath
all the religions, all the faiths, and all the philoso-
phies : in a word, beneath all the visible and everyday manifestations of human thought." He thinks
it hardly to be contested that this source is to be
found in ancient India. Thence he says, "in all
probability the sacred teaching spread into Egypt,
found its way to ancient Persia and Chaldea, per-
meated the Hebrew race, and crept into Greece and
the north of Europe, finally reaching China and
even America, where the Aztec civilization was
merely a more or less distorted reproduction of the
Egyptian civilization."

So "The Great Secret" which Maeterlinck in-
quires into is a concern of religion and of the
knowledge that built cities and raised monuments,
the remains of which we find in tropical jungles
and dig up from the sands of deserts—a process

that is going on more and more all the time as
money and men can be spared to do it, and the
results of which are nowadays examined and interpreted in a fashion that is highly edifying.

But some old monuments of the first quality
have stood up in plain sight since anything like
modern times began. The most notable of them is
that Pyramid of Cheops which our correspondent
speaks of. Maeterlinck has his say about it. He
calls it "a sort of stupendous hieroglyph, which,
by its dimensions, its proportions, its internal ar-
rangements, and its astronomical orientation,
propounds a whole series of riddles of which only
the most obvious have hitherto been deciphered.
. . . An occult tradition," he says, "had always
affirmed that this pyramid contained essential secrets, but only quite recently has anyone begun to
discover them." It has been discovered that the
line running north and south through the apex of
the pyramid is the ideal meridian crossing the
greatest amount of land and the smallest amount
of sea; that the height of the pyramid multiplied
by one million is almost precisely the distance of
the earth from the sun accepted by modern astronomers; that the polar radius of the earth divided by ten million is precisely the cubit that was
the unit of measure of the pyramid builders; that
their inch multiplied by one hundred million is
the distance the earth travels in one day, and that
the entrance passage of the pyramid pointed to
the pole star at the time it was built. So much,

relating to astronomy, has been gathered from the signs of past knowledge which that pyramid gives, and that much, at least, is a sort of information that can be verified with a tape measure by anybody who has the requisite knowledge and time to spare.

Maeterlinck thinks it very remarkable that none of the hieroglyphs that have been deciphered make any reference to all this extraordinary knowledge which is built into that pyramid. He infers that the old-time priests, who knew these things, did not advertise but kept them quiet. That is where our times are different. Everything gets into the papers except what the War Department knows about new war gases, and intimations leak out even about them. But the old-time priests seem to have felt that a little knowledge was a dangerous thing, and probably as to the knowledge they had they were right. They seem to have known very curious things: how to direct lightning; how to send instantaneous messages from temple to temple, no matter how far—and even in the time of Moses (which was only the day before yesterday) they could compete with Aaron at least as effectively as Houdini can compete with Mrs. Crandon.

As to the age of that pyramid there is a considerable conflict of opinion. It is called the Pyramid of Cheops and it is also called the great Pyramid of Ghizeh—the name of the place where it stands. Possibly Cheops was somebody whom archæologists think they know about and can place in time, but the Theosophists do much better than that: they put that pyramid back thirty thousand years and say it belongs to the really great period of Egypt's greatness, before the last big Atlantean island was swallowed up overnight with a loss of sixty-four million lives—which beats even the record of the motor cars to-day. That engulfing of the last of Atlantis produced high water in Egypt—so they say—and they think this ancient pyramid was under water for a few thousand years and came up again when the land rose and the sea of Sahara was tipped out and left us the present desert.

One likes that story better than those the archæologists tell. It has larger features and it accounts for the silence of the Egyptian hieroglyphs which puzzles Maeterlinck. Why play favorites so much about what is so? The story of Atlantis, which used to be a fable forty years ago, is getting more respectable every day. It accounts for so much. A prevalent notion is that the really ancient knowledge of Egypt grew up in Atlantis and spilled over into Egypt at one end and into Central America and this continent generally at the other. Mexico, we are told, is a very ancient land, habitable since long, long ago, and this information seems really to be valid and supported by geology. We must get used to the idea of enormous geographical changes which upset the ancient peoples very seriously. The tradition of the flood possibly derives from the immersion of that last big island which was left of the continent of Atlantis, and the contemporaneous antics of what is now the Mediterranean Sea.

A. P. Sinnett, the Theosophist, though relying
on theosophical processes for information about the
prehistoric world, drops into what he calls "commonplace testimony of the ordinary kind" about
the discoveries of Doctor Le Plongeon, a French
archæologist in Mexico. Le Plongeon lived and
worked in Mexico many years, Mr. Sinnett says,
and was the first to decipher the Mexican hiero-
glyphics. He succeeded in translating what archæologists know as the Troano manuscript, a very
ancient Mexican writing which he found to contain
a straightforward narrative of the submergence
of Atlantis, which catastrophe, the manuscript
says, took place "8,060 years before the writing of
this book." That is definite if true, and possibly
some learned person with his feet on the ground
knows about this Troano manuscript. Colonel Cabanas in Spain, who searches into these matters,
says (as quoted from a psychic journal of Costa
Rica, *Claros de Luna*, which in turn is quoted by
Light, of London) that the British Museum contains some writings found in Mexico which treat
of the sinking of Atlantis. This Señor Cabanas,
who is working on the Atlantis problem, is described as a Lieutenant Colonel of Engineers who
has psychic faculties himself and works with a
clairvoyant medium. A Spanish journal, *Diario
del Comercio*, has a report of a conversation he
had with King Alfonso in which he describes his
method—which is to get an inviting archæological
object out of one of the Spanish Museums and
invite the medium, Aguilar, to tell about it. Agui-

lar tells very remarkable tales which, it seems, have interested Flammarion. The idea of a clair-voyant medium getting a story out of an object is not novel but is an exercise of which spiritist records give many curious examples; but to go back to the Stone Age and antediluvian times seems a considerable stretch of this interesting faculty.

How the Theosophists get the information about very ancient proceedings in which they put so much confidence can doubtless be ascertained by reading their textbooks, of which there is no lack; but they hold, so it seems, that the great pyramid is contemporaneous with the last days of Atlantis and has in it the evidences of knowledge and of powers which presently disappeared from earth. One of the stories about the pyramid is of the ascending passage so contrived as to be a record of prophecy of things due to happen in this world down to our time and somewhat beyond it. The group of earnest people who interest themselves in the theory that the English and others are de-scendants of the Lost Tribes lean hard on the great pyramid as a part of the basis of their belief, and have great confidence in the interpretation of the prophecies said to have been built into the ascend-ing passage. They are all figured out up to date. They tell us that they indicated with great accu-racy the dates of the beginning and end of the great World War, and warn us that we have trou-bles still to come and tell us precisely when to expect them, but assure us that with good luck our civilization will survive.

The usefulness of the occultists, if there is any, seems to be to remind us that this world is not so commonplace as most of us matter-of-fact people suppose. Human life is a very extraordinary thing. Human knowledge is still in the infant class. Human conduct is not yet wisely enough directed to give much assurance of permanence. Human powers are in a process of development of which the end is nowhere in sight.

Has enough been said to fill, in any degree, the order of our correspondent in the English colony? Can the suggestions above cited of the great antiquity of civilization, the intimations of knowledge possessed and lost, the suggestion of new knowledge now in the making and scornfully rejected by the cocksure—can such things serve to check the vainglory of Americans who see in current knowledge and current exploits the culmination of the efforts of the human mind? Probably not, but let them do what they can. Anybody who thinks this is a know-it-all age will think so until he learns better, but the great scientists already do know better. So do the great doctors and even the great statesmen. They all know that what we know is not all, nor yet enough. The doctors do wonderful things, but the wise ones know that there are secrets of cure, secrets of disease, secrets of energy which are still beyond them. As for the electricians, they are in the position that they do not know where they "get off." They are dealing with a force the nature of which they do not understand. They increase in understanding of what it will do, how it can be harnessed, how it can be used, but not much in knowing what it is. When they get beyond a certain point of practical application, their theories and those of some of the occultists show signs of merging. The statesmen and the politicians are at a loss how to manage the world so as to save it from self-destruction. They do their best, but the best of them wonder if their knowledge is equal to their job. Theologians dispute; organized religion suffers criticism; ministers turn from the spiritual to the material application of religion, and the reason of it all is that they do not know enough about the origin and purpose of human life.

This is a great age. It is uncommonly learned. It builds, contrives, acquires, and speculates with extraordinary activity, but it is far from being the only great age this venerable world has seen, and it is still a good way from the assurance—so desirable—that it knows enough to discover for itself the pathway to salvation.

World's End and Meanwhile

APRIL 1925

HAT THE APRIL NUMBER OF THIS MAGA-
zine comes out may be accepted as a sign
that the world did not come to an end on
the sixth of February, as was so confidently expected by a few people, and so widely advertised
in the newspapers. Predictions of the end of the
world almost always disappoint expectation. Apparently people can compute eclipses. We have
all seen eclipses which they predicted and we know
that they were true to the time-table. But as to
the end of the world there has been no one who
has guessed right since Noah, for that was sub-
stantially what Noah predicted. The world did
not exactly end, but it did end for the people whom
Noah knew about, except those who sailed with
him.

Somehow the Flood has been coming nearer to
us. It says in the Bible that it rained for forty
days and nights—and no doubt it did rain—but
according to contemporary judgment the main job
of causing a large-sized flood is handled by geo-
logical disturbances: continents sinking, continents
rising; water spilled off here, water shut in there;
a new arrangement of land, and of course a lot of
people drowned. Nobody seems to object very
much in these times to relating Noah's flood to
the sinking of a continent like Atlantis, or some-

thing of that sort. There was a flood. Noah with
due notice might have built a ship and out-floated
his world, as the Bible says. Theoretically it was
possible. How much of the Bible story is fact
and how much is legend it is not easy to say, except
for a Fundamentalist, but in the main it looks like
a story based in fact, for we practically know
that, first and last, the end of the world has come
for many, many people on this earth.

One may wonder how Noah's contemporaries
bore it. It must have been quite like the loss of
the *Titanic*. Were there folks on rafts in Noah's
time who commented on Noah, and criticized him?
No doubt there were. It is hard to think of any
eye-witness of the Flood from outside of the Ark
taking a cheerful or even a reasonably philosophical view of it. It was trying. Even Noah himself, after it was all over, felt the need of relaxation. Of course it was wet, probably stormy.
People on rafts or in tree tops would get so mis-
erable physically, from wet clothes and lack of
creature comforts, that their spirits would be much
affected by it. But theoretically the prospect of
the end of the world ought not to bother any really
well-informed person, for it would be a great rid-
dance of troublesome problems and people. It is
just as Emerson said to the Millerite who told
him the world would end in ten days: "No doubt
we shall get along just as well without it." We
ought to, and when we realize that we ought to,
perhaps we shall be better able to endure the

vicissitudes and imperfections of a world still with us, and widely felt to be too much so.

One of the encouraging signs of the times is the great prevalence of dissatisfaction with life as it is lived. There is an immense amount of action, particularly organized action, and vast differences of opinion as to whether most of it is doing any good. The Drys have moved heaven and earth to stay the flow of rum, and the Wets are sure that the harm which has been done by limiting free will and bringing law into contempt far more than offsets the gains of unwilling abstinence. In politics nowadays there is a more novel ailment than the ordinary ruction between opposed parties, to wit, the suspicion grown widespread that neither party is much good, and that government itself is such an imperfect instrument that there ought to be a consultation of doctors about it.

Where is all that fury of sentiment which finally developed over Mr. Wilson and the League of Nations? There is nothing like that now on any subject. Most of the leading promoters of it are dead, and those who remain talk to yawning listeners. Things are not going badly. These States are not failing altogether just now in their duty to Europe. They are furnishing money in useful quantities to that continent. They have sent extremely good men over there to render specific services. The way they have accomplished it has done us credit, but as for a general, all-pervading interest in anything— even in Europe—it does not exist. What interest there is runs to details. Hereabouts there is a vast deal of building going on: road building, cathedral building, immense construction of abodes for schools and colleges, also of human habitations. The minds of men seem to have got away from general ideas and to be fastened just now on particulars.

Perhaps that is just as well. There is a time for all things and this seems to be the time for organization and construction. When we are carried away by a great idea and have a big job on our hands—as we had in the War—construction goes to grass. Everything not necessary to the accomplishment of the great purpose is cut out. The construction that is going on now is partly a War result. Besides that, there is another aspect of it: when people's nerves are bad, doctors set them to work with their hands. That is soothing and helpful; it applies to the ordinary routine of life; we all feel more or less the need to do something with our hands that we may the better do something with our heads. Manual training and golf are forms of recognition of that need. Society builds and organizes because use must be found for idle energy and idle money. Presently there may come along something that will sweep through all this construction and give purpose and motive to it. Do you remember how in the War days, as one traveled or drove about the country, he took a new notice of mills and factories and the accumulated apparatus of our civilization as so much power to win the War? So we go on now accumulating apparatus, for ends that are not clear yet, but which certainly has some sort of destined use.

For civilization does really require a very considerable apparatus. We are not yet stocked up as well as Europe with objects interesting and stimulating to look at. We ought to be, and at the present rate of construction it will not be long before we are. We cannot provide ourselves with antiquity over night, but time works ceaselessly and will fetch antiquity without extra charge if only we make due provision of objects proper to become antiquated.

Meanwhile all this constructive effort does not go on without outcries. The big New York cathedral, whereof the building has started up again so prosperously, seems to some people entirely out of date—a useless fabrication not adapted to our day nor to twentieth-century needs. But, of course, nothing so handsome as that cathedral will be when it is finished is ever useless. For beauty's sake alone it is worth the effort it calls for, and it may serve a very valuable turn in increasing unity among all varieties of religious people.

Consider the case of Harvard College, which for fifty years past has been trying to keep its place in a rapidly growing country. Fifty years ago it was a college of national renown. In that half century colleges and universities have multiplied in the land, received immense endowments or liberal allowances of tax money, and taken strong

root, and old colleges which had no special advantages of some kind have lost in relative importance. Those that were not willing to take
that loss have had to bestir themselves, and they
have bestirred themselves. They have spread their
organizations in the West; they have vastly increased their endowments. In fifty years most of
them have quadrupled or more in size and they
are still adding, scrambling for more money, or-
ganizing their graduates, advertising by their
prowess in sports, and all the time building and
undertaking new exploits in education. In all that
they are like the rest of the country—some of them
a little ahead of it. As for Harvard, one hears
that it is full of dispute, that a certain proportion
of its graduates are very dissatisfied with what it
is now doing—that everything about it is criticized: its new Business School; its loss of Mr.
Baker, the dramatic teacher, who was carried off by
Yale; its recent deficiencies in the major sports; the
disposition to put the standard up a little so as to
reduce the number of lazy scholars. That college
was the loser last year in all the major sports.
Graduates who are chiefly interested in those concerns are sure the University is in a most unhealthy state. The loss of Mr. Baker produced a
violent eruption of criticism. The gift of a large
endowment to the Business School by another Mr.
Baker, not yet a member of the Harvard faculty,
suggested to a considerable cohort of observers
that Harvard was turning to materialism and that
the concerns of the mind and spirit were on the

way to take places subordinate to more practical
and material details of knowledge. Apparently
the gentlemen who have been organized for purposes of money getting and construction have
come to feel, not unnaturally, that their wishes
must count for something in the administration
of the University. And so discussion abounds
in Cambridge and about it, and what does it all
come to? Simply to this: that construction there
and in the Boston district has come to a point where
discussion has naturally broken out about what it
is all for. What sort of life, what sort of character, what sort of ability shall all these vast endowments and buildings and organizations aim at?

That same question lies ahead for all of us. Here
we are building all sorts of things, improving all
the means of communication, piling up money, piling up education as we understand it, accumulating
even knowledge, and driving straight on toward
discussion of the question—what is it all about,
what sort of a life are we planning for, what basis
has it, and shall we like it when we get it?

Every rich country can build; every rich country
has built. The world abounds in such construction, some of it in ruins, some of it underground,
some of it handsome but inoperative, a great deal
of it still useful and busy. Building will go on
and so will expansion. If there is money they
always do. They went on in Germany for thirty
years before the War to a marvelous extent.
Some time since they went on in Nineveh, Baby-
lon, India, Egypt, China, Africa, Ceylon, Yucatan,

Mexico, and various parts of South America. It is a dull week for the newspapers nowadays that does not announce the discovery of some forgotten city. Thus, building is more or less instinctive and inevitable. It comes along when the means to do it are available. The great question for us is whether our turn at it will produce something which will endure, and whether human life will prosper in the apparatus we are contriving for it; whether, in short, the soul of man will profit by that apparatus, or the contrary.

That is the whole question—the soul of man. If the soul prospers the apparatus will keep going and do good. If it does not, the apparatus will go to pot. In Germany, so lately, the apparatus was wonderful. It included a certain kind of learning, very remarkable in its department. But the soul did not prosper. That country put its entire trust in its apparatus and presently it fell down with a very heavy jolt—one, indeed, that shook the world. We do not want any more of those jolts; especially we do not want them here. In this large, fairly comfortable continent a thousand years of progressive life is a moderate expectation. We have a great deal, we are getting more all the time, but we are far from being in agreement about what we are headed for, whether we ought to get there, whether the means we are using are helpful to get us where we ought to go. They say of Harvard College just now that it is full of blocs, each of which sees its own interest big and wants to be sure that it gets its share of

the common fund. That is also the way of the
country at large—it is full of blocs, no one of
which wants any other bloc to get ahead of it.
Very well; and what is the remedy? Is it in
more organization, more money raising, more construction, more and better machines, more "education," as the training for all these activities is now
called?

No. God, who was not in the whirlwind, the
earthquake, or the fire is not in the factory or the
machine shop, or in salesmanship or advertisement. He remains, as heretofore, in the still small
voice. Organization, construction, and all those
useful things are like the operations of the body.
When they need to be quickened or corrected or
improved in some way, the doctors (if they are
skilful) can usually do it. But when you see
sick people to whom the doctors can bring nothing
better than alleviation, and often not even that,
then you say they need an infusion of new life and
you wonder how they are going to get it. Sometimes they do get it and you see them get well,
and recover energy, and go on and finish their
course.

And so it is with the world. Organization and
all that may benefit it but won't cure it. The cure
has got to come from something that will increase
knowledge and revive faith. Such succor to a
troubled world usually has come from irregular
and even disputable sources, and it may do so
again.

In Extenuation of the Incredible

OCTOBER 1925

HE IMPRESSION I GET," SAID COLOPHON, "is that some people sometimes cure in some people almost any disease that there is. I don't find myself in agreement with the boundaries you doctors put to the diseases that can be cured by mental or spiritual means."

"They can't cure cancer," said Dimity. "I know about cancer. I deal with him in my business. You've got to cut him out, and do it root and branch. There is no other way. When you've done it a healer may help the cure perhaps if they really do help anything, but they can't cure cancer."

"Oh, well; of course, Bill, I don't know cancer as you do. Pathologically—if that's the word—I don't know anything about it. All I know is what I read in the papers and what comes in the mail. Those are my great sources of information, to be supplemented on occasion, as now, by talk with the knowledgeful. For observe, that the things you ought most to talk about are the things you know least about—contrary to prevalent supposition—because so talking you may get information."

"Yes, you may, but you ain't very apt to, and maybe that's why people usually feel about talk that the Bible's right and it is better to give than to receive. But of course, Colly, when you get a

chance to talk cancer to an expert like me who
knows about it, you're lucky."

"Knows about it! Go 'long! Say 'Knows
something about it': that's about as much as anyone can say of anything. *You* know cancer? No!
All you know is how to cut 'em out. I don't doubt
you know that, and if I had one I'd employ you.
But here are newspapers, letters, pamphlets, periodicals, and books providing mountains of testimony that cancer is being cured all the time by
saints, healers, Christian Scientists, marvel workers,
Unity practitioners working from Kansas City,
and Heaven knows who else."

"But, Colly, you don't really believe all that
trash, do you? Surely you don't believe the stories
you read in the papers about cures!"

"Some of them! Some of them! At least I
contemplate them and keep them in mind for reflection and further reference, and to see what
turns up that seems to have a bearing on them."

"Do you believe the testimonials that go with
the patent-medicine advertisements?"

"I don't bother with them: The proportion of
lies that one must expect in them is too high. But
these Unity, Christian Science, healer, saint's-shrine
and other religious cures are a little different.
Even patent-medicine is medicine, but those mental
and spiritual cures are something else, and something with an extended historical background behind it. The tradition of cures by these various
immaterial means is about as old as anything in
human record."

"Oh, yes! there are these cases, of course, but not cancer."

"Perhaps not cancer. I don't remember any case of a lost limb made to grow again. Possibly cancer is like that. But I don't understand it so. I think of it as something that bites and grows and must be reached and killed or removed in some way. And of course what you say about it is practically right and the thing you ought to say. But what we are really talking about isn't cancer at all, but how much you know. You see, I can't imagine a really first-class marvel worker turning away from cancer as something too much for him as easily as I can imagine a limit to your knowledge of the means to check disease in the body. You don't think everything is known yet about the body and how to deal with it, do you?"

"Lord, no! In medicine, and most things else, the surface has been scratched; that's all. The more any doctor learns, the more aware he must become of the regions his knowledge does not reach. But still, we know a lot more than we did even thirty years ago, and the new knowledge seems to come faster and faster, and certainly comes in very handy."

"Sure! Now you've said all I ask of you. You admit you know comparatively little, and when you say cancer can't be cured by mental or spiritual means, it means that in your present state of knowledge you cannot conceive of such cures. Now you understand a knife. You know how to use it and what can be done with it. But do you think you understand the means by which mental and spiritual cures are effected?"

"Oh, well, in a way one understands suggestion. No good doctor nowadays ignores the power of the mind over the body! But it won't cure cancer."

"I suppose not. To cure cancer you must have, I should say, an agent that will penetrate tissue like X-rays or radium, and destroy cells, and extirpate whatever you call the creatures which do the mischief. You need something that will do what a knife or radium will do, and much more. This agent must be usable by some will which under right conditions can send it on its errand and make it do its job. By means of such an agent it seems to me—a very ignorant man and likely to be mistaken—that cancer might be cured."

"Possibly! Possibly! Why deny that the impossible may not be achieved by the unimaginable? But do you think, Colly, that such a force as you describe exists and can be handled?"

"I suspect it does exist, and that now and then someone comes along who is able to handle it. Sir Oliver Lodge defines it in a way when in writing of Doctor Geley, who lately died, he says Geley had in mind 'a dynamic power of the mental and spiritual regions competent to control, guide and rearrange atoms of matter.' I am so constituted, and so impressed by what I have read or heard, as to believe that most of the Bible stories of miracles, both Old Testament and New, are true, and that they constitute a record which shows us what is possible. The cures in the two Testaments are of much the same sort. Leprosy was cured both by Elisha and by Christ. I don't know what leprosy is and how it compares with cancer; but it has usually beaten the doctors, though one reads that our medical men have lately got a line on it in the Philippines. And for that matter one reads of a new line on cancer disclosed in England, but pirated, the latest rumor says, from Germany. So of bringing the dead, or apparently dead, to life. Elijah brought back the widow's son, and Elisha, the child of the Shunamite; Christ raised Lazarus. I don't remember cures in the Old Testament of expulsion of devils and restoration of crazy people to sanity, but outside of cures there is a likeness between the exploit of the widow's inexhaustible cruse and barrel of meal and the multiplication of bread and fishes in the feeding of the multitudes. I have read that this multiplication of food is done now in the East but that men who can do it are of a sort that does not advertise, and that they do not disclose their accomplishment except on very special occasions. Then there's levitation of one kind or another, and, oh, do you remember the story of a man who lost his ax-head into the Jordan, which Elisha kindly made float for him? How do you suppose he did that?"

"You may search me! Gosh! Colly, do you believe all that, and go about without an attendant and have a license to drive motor cars? Isn't it

easier for you to believe that the boy lied than
that Elisha made iron float?"

"No, bless you! No! It doesn't seem to me
much of a stunt for a party with the powers of
Elisha to make iron float. Why should you feel
it to be so much more incredible than Miss Tarbell's story of how Mr. Morgan and Judge Gary
floated the Steel Trust? Now, there was really
a big job in making metals float. And accomplished how? Simply by the action of the human
mind. No force employed; no knock down or drag
out; but simply mental forces—imagination,
strength of will; not precisely the forces by which
the so-called miracles are done, but something very
close to them. Did you read how Mr. Morgan
and Judge Gary finally constrained John Gates
to take what they offered him? Beautiful! Like
a poker story!"

"Fine story! oh, yes! but not the same kind of
story as of the ax-head that swam."

"Oh, well, the main difference is that you don't
know enough to understand the ax-head story,
whereas the John Gates story comes within scope
of your knowledge. If you knew more, I dare
say you'd think Miss Tarbell's story was the
greater wonder of the two."

"I think, Colly, you're just another Fundamentalist like Bryan. You seem ready to believe all
these Bible stories."

"Sure! I do believe most of them; not merely
because they are in the Bible, but because I think
they are probably true, or at least based on sub-

stantial truth. As far as belief goes, I don't think Bryan could have bettered me much, but to me the Bible is a great stimulant to research, whereas Bryan seemed inclined to use it as a limitation on research. It makes me want to know, and whereas Bryan seemed always fearful that someone would find out something which didn't match with something the Bible said, that never worries me at all. I like to know what the Bible is and how it was compounded, and I do not understand how a man so clever in certain ways as Bryan was should have taken the view that it was a kind of coffer-dam, with the walls of which it was not safe to meddle for fear they would spring a leak and let all their contents out. Somehow you got him scared—you fellows, Bill, you doctors and scientists. Knowing what he did and believing what he did, and feeling the importance of his belief in what he did believe, he could see where you fell down; but, because either of the limitations of his mind or of his knowledge, he could not avoid that impossible position about the Bible. Still, I think, his showdown was better than Darrow's. Don't you?"

"I'd hardly say that. I wasn't rapturous about Darrow, but still he had understanding of a lot of things that Bryan didn't understand at all."

"Oh, yes, but he showed a total lack of understanding of a lot of things that Bryan did understand, and which were more important than the others. Bryan was out of date in some of his notions about the Bible and in his feeling that if one admitted that anywhere in it there was a flaw in inspiration or a deviation from fact, the divine authority of the whole book would be destroyed and faith in the religion it stands for would go to grass. That is not so, and it was surprisingly simple of him to feel about it as he did, though millions of people in this country see it about as he did, and make these views of his the basis of acclaiming him as a defender of the Faith—which must make the angels reach for their pocket handkerchiefs. But Darrow proclaimed himself agnostic, without settled convictions about religion, or even about what is commonly called immortality, meaning the survival of personality after the body dies. Bryan at least appeared in court in a suit of clothes, though you may not like the cut of it, but Darrow was in rags, and seemed to feel they did him credit."

"He gave greater evidence of intelligence than Bryan did. He made a holy show of Bryan with the questions he asked of him."

"It isn't a sign of intelligence to believe nothing. It's a sign of defect. You don't send agnostics to hospitals to be cured of their disability because hospitals can't cure them but, if they could, a good many of them might apply to be sent, for there are plenty of agnostics who mislike their own state. To believe in man but not in immortality is like believing in fishes but not in water. Mr. Darrow is probably not overpleased to be in that condition. The theory of evolution is part of a study of processes. Bryan was agnostic as to that theory, but Darrow was agnostic about the results of the evolution he defended. He admitted his uncertainty whether anything of importance had been evolved. If man blows out for good when his wick separates from his tallow, evolution, if it is true, is of no tremendous concern for us, though it may serve a turn in providing entertainment to our Creator; but if life, begun or continued on earth, proceeds elsewhere in the invisible, to more or less advantage according as time has been well or ill used, evolution seems more important.

"We have to live a good deal in the imagination to get along at all. Bryan must have lived so. If Darrow doesn't, he is a loser. But probably he does, for even he is intelligent. And it should be remembered that his errand at Dayton was not to upset belief, but to hinder impediments from being put in the way of the pursuit of truth. I would rather have had that errand in the keeping of someone who had a conscious vision of more truth than Darrow had. Malone was better about that. He had belief enough.

"For belief, Bill, which is Faith, so much commended for its power to move things—is an enormous asset, even when it includes confidence in some things that are not so. Indeed, in everyone who has it, it must include such imperfections, because our knowledge is so limited. We believe what we can get of what has come through in our time, and our spiritual beliefs are more or less affected by the achievements of the searchers of our day in the departments of physical knowledge.

The torch bearers get wonderful things by intuition, inspiration, or spiritual means of one sort or another, but their news is apt to lag in general acceptance until what we know as scientific knowledge gets far enough along to make it credible. It took a hundred years or so for the theories of Copernicus and Galileo to become respectable. At the start the pious and the powerful rejected them and put Galileo in jail. That is a regular process with great innovations of theory. But in these times things move faster, and new knowledge is not so easily squelched.

"Moreover the wonderful acceleration of discovery in the physical realm is bound to help us to a fuller understanding of the spiritual department. Wireless and radio and all such things; electricity, electrons, the last new thing and the next one, extend our powers of belief. And that is a good thing, for most people will agree that vastly more things are so than we think are so, and that limitless crops of truth stand waiting to be gathered from fields still uncut."

Since They Buried Fitzpatrick

HEN DID OLD TIMES END AND THE NEW era begin? . . . In 1914? . . . Before that! . . . With the beginning of the new century?

One would say a little earlier. Somehow, in the mind of the Easy Chair it is associated with Fitzpatrick's funeral. The exact year of the funeral matters not, but it was in the summer, along somewhere in the late '90s, and the picture of it going by on a dusty road as one looked out of the window of a book-lined study in the old house in Owasco, is for some reason extraordinarily vivid in the mind—a long, long succession of buggies and farmers' light wagons filing by after the mortal remnants of Fitzpatrick; summer, sunshine and dust, and a sense that the affection and regard the funeral showed was all well due, and earned by benefits conferred.

Fitzpatrick was a butcher; doubtless an Irishman; probably a Catholic, else why should his funeral have been proceeding down the road past our house to the town where there was a Catholic church and cemetery? He lived somewhere up the lake, in Sempronius maybe, for Owasco is in classical New York. Somewhere in that neighborhood our fellow citizen John D. Rockefeller spent his boyhood and first began to practice the art

200

of acquisition in which he has won such great renown. Not so Fitzpatrick. He did nothing momentous in that line. He was a butcher, as said, an active, hearty man, who came down the road two or three times a week on his meat wagon, supplying animal food to households and taking a lively and benevolent interest in the concerns of his fellow creatures. A very good man, who lived a life of service, as was attested by that long line of farmer vehicles trailing along after a hearse on a dusty road on a summer day.

In '96 or '97 that must have been. Perhaps the Spanish War was going on. Anyhow, it was imminent, and that was the beginning of the new times.

My gracious! Consider what changes thirty years have wrought in this world and in human life!

A new era has undoubtedly come, but no one can say yet where it is coming out. The more one regards it, the more uncertain he must be as to the details of its development.

We may have ever so much faith that human life is progressing to a better phase and yet be left full of speculations as to the immediate processes of that progress. The truth is they do not look particularly engaging, though the efforts at Locarno were encouraging.

Consider war! The world has had war, was for a time quite seriously oversupplied with it; is quite positive that it does not want any more; is pretty sure that it is an extremely expensive cure and very likely to kill the patient, and yet it does not know how to get rid of it. It is in a most curious state about that. Everybody is afraid that there will be another big fight and nobody, except the Quakers, wants to get into it barehanded. Along with the vision of a new world and new conditions of life go the compulsions and the considerations of the old world and the old conditions. The habit of carrying a gun is extremely strong in nations. The public sentiment of the world is that nobody should go armed except the policemen, but no general rule to that effect has yet been contrived.

And there is morals and there is religion, neither of them in a very satisfactory case: crimes of violence abounding, divorce very prevalent; the law not respected, and in the opinion of many good minds not respectable; the churches and their members involved in creedal disputes, and not at all pleased with themselves nor with one another' quite aware that things are not going with them as they should; suspicious that they have lost something and very perplexed where to look for it.

"Youth is on the loose," says a book reviewer, "because the tribal *mores* are in collapse. The adult has lost his relentless faith in right and wrong, a thousand new influences are at work in the child's environment—the comic strips, the 'movies,' the headlines, post-war cynicism, advertising, increasing city congestion—and single inviolable standards have given way to a confusing multiplicity of standards. The old handholds are rotten and the new ones have not been forged." So says Mr. Stuart Chase, described as "of the New York Labor Bureau," reviewing a couple of books in the Sunday *Tribune's* literary supplement.

Prohibition is not dead, neither is it particularly thriving. The Federal Council of Churches has reviewed it punctiliously and at length, and said in effect that it was languishing and needed tonics. Maybe it needs a drink. Certainly it is not giving much satisfaction even to its adherents and supporters. The main discussion about it is whether it can be helped by modification.

But that is uncertain like everything else—like the foreign debts, for example. Great Britain has arranged for the payment of her debt to us and her payments are coming in, but they do not give any great degree of satisfaction. A lot of people here squirm about it and are afraid that England cannot afford what she is paying nor we to receive what we are taking. There is no great peace of mind about these payments, nor will there be about other payments so long as they come out of countries heavily burdened with obligations and hampered by a great falling off of trade. If the countries that owe us money came jointly to the counting room with bags of it gathered out of their prosperity and turned it in with thanks for the accommodation, that would be one thing; but nothing like that is going on at all. All payments are made more or

less under protest and the gratitude of mankind
to us at present is almost exclusively the sense
of favors to come, especially of loans. It is a
grand thing to be unpopular in a good cause but
less felicitous to be so when one is worried for
fear he is not doing entirely right.

Also connected with the foreign debts is the
glaring fact that if paid at all they must be paid
by imports from the countries that owe them. The
fear of imports is always strong in our manufacturers, and we run a tariff up sky high against
the very payments we arrange for. And there is
every prospect that we shall run it up higher if
our manufacturers find themselves in competition
with the cheaper labor of debt-paying Europe.
Somehow it seems neither good sense nor good
morals to insist upon repayments and at the same
time build up a wall against them. All that one
can hope is that payments in goods will not be
abundant enough to raise the tariff wall extortion-
ately and increase in serious measure the prices
of things we have to buy.

Then there is the curious disturbance over evolution, considerably mixed up, sad to say, with
politics. It was the same way with Prohibition.
The people who wanted Prohibition put it into
politics as strongly as they could. So the anti-
evolutionists, who insist that evolution is contrary
to the accepted theories of religion, are ready to
organize against candidates who do not take that
view. Undoubtedly there is coming a restatement
of the religious belief of religious people in our

day. So much news has come to the world about
so many things, and so much more is coming so
fast, that the old statements which were good in
their day, do not hold the contemporary mind.
There is no true conflict between different statements of truth, but there is plenty of conflict between half truths, and that is what is going on
now.

B Y MACHINERY and by the great development of
what we call education, and by the immense increase of the powers of man over material things we
have made enormous gains in efficiency, but we have
not gained equally in tolerance. That is the main
trouble with us and the cure for it is more knowledge, and especially more knowledge of spiritual
things. The efficiency of man is increased by what
is taught in the schools—reading, writing, arithme-
tic, chemistry, physics, and all the sciences, but no
increase of knowledge in those subjects alone will
save the world or bring peace to it, for one may be
skilled in all those matters and yet have no true
conception of the purpose of human life and the
spiritual laws that govern us.

Materialism—says a current writer—is bankrupt as a practical philosophy of conduct. In its practical working it is not
a philosophical theory but a habit of mind. Its effects are
always disastrous because it reduces morality to convention.
It always degenerates into Epicureanism and regards Religion
as a dope for the masses in the interests of property. It
removes God from the world, makes the human will the only
arbiter of conduct, exalts selfishness (enlightened or otherwise)
as the only rule of life, and the logical result never fails to work

out in conflicts and the dominance of brute force. It was so in Greece, in Rome and in Judæa, and there are plenty of modern examples of the same sequences, both international and social. This ignoring of the actual and inevitable result of the Law of Spiritual Consequences which is the real governance of God, is exceedingly common at the present day. Whole classes in every nation act as though God were a negligible quantity. It is this forgetfulness which moved the warnings of the Hebrew prophets, and it invariably works out in national disaster just because the moral law is as much a part of the constitution of the universe as gravitation.

That is a good statement (by Stanley De Brath) of what ails our world at the present time. It is a picture of the slough we are in and it suggests the true reason for the embarrassment of us Americans about those foreign debts. It is a habit of our minds to consider that borrowed money must be repaid. So, as a rule, it must, but there is a higher law about it, and that we do not seem capable of comprehending or applying. But events may apply it and in ways we shall not like by consequences that will be both painful and expensive and so, possibly, we shall learn.

In great crises, so long as they last, selfish habits of mind seem to dissolve. When San Francisco was shaken down and burned up everyone for a time seemed to look after everybody else. So it was very considerably in the War. So it is when floods drive antagonistic animals to hilltops. They don't fight one another while the waters are high, but when the waters subside, the animals return again to their hereditary antagonisms, and dog and cat dispute as before. Must it be that this world is to fall again into torment before the nations finally learn to be brotherly to one another? That is really the great question of the time; whether we can learn soon enough to be good to avert a lot more punishment, or whether we are so stupid that our heads must be knocked together, our treasures wasted, and hearts broken again by wholesale bereavement? No one knows the answer to that question. We have gained in efficiency and lost in tolerance. Somehow we must make up that loss; somehow we must get better understanding of what life is about and of what Mr. De Brath calls the Law of Spiritual Consequences, which is the real governance of God.

The means to do so are not lacking. The quest for saving spiritual knowledge was never keener than it is now, never pressed more resolutely, and never with richer and more astonishing results. Not in all our concerns are the blind leading the blind. There are those who see and practice constantly to see better; who find a message worth giving and give it. In all religious companies and outside of organized religion altogether, one finds such people, and the pith of their messages is the same. The world is by no means going out in darkness. On the contrary it never was more conscious of light ahead, and never more eager to reach it. Its necessities compel that eagerness, and if it seems to lag, as it does, it is only because the critical state of its affairs seem so urgently to demand haste.

So they do, but no living man can make a time-table for mankind. The best he can do is to try to increase and diffuse true intelligence, for according to the true intelligence of men is their behavior, and according to their behavior events befall.

Current Civilization

HEADLINE IN THE NEWSPAPER AN-nounces that "Motor Traffic Chokes De-troit." That city, it seems, is unable to find due street room for cars. The city fathers are widening the avenues and a hundred million dollar program, extending over fifteen years, is suggested as a remedy.

That makes a picture in the mind of what is happening in this expansive and incidentally, very expensive civilization in which we are struggling. We all know that they make automobiles in De-troit. It is a specialty of that town and the city takes its own medicine. The paper which has the headline says, "almost everyone in Detroit drives," and that everyone with even five dollars as a first payment is a potential buyer of a car. About 200,000 persons out of Detroit's population of 1,200,000 are said to be employed in automobile factories and, not only make cars, but ride in them. Naturally, the main streets of the town are con-gested. The specialty that has "made" Detroit has also embarrassed it. The streets are not wide enough and there are not garages enough to hold the cars, so that "all night parking" is remarked as a growing factor, and highborn and shiny cars stand out in the streets in the night watches with their humbler brethren.

The rulers of the city take all kinds of thought about the situation, and talk about streets 120 feet wide and, indeed, have actually planned to make some streets super-highways 204 feet wide, which would give traveling room for eight cars abreast, four going each way. There is a Master Plan, the one calling for one hundred million dollars in fifteen years that Detroit thinks may possibly make the going more comfortable, but would it?

We all know this story more or less, know it intimately in New York. It is a very expensive story. We see the avenues widening and all extra space won for the cars by squeezing the tax payers, instantly gobbled up by more cars. We notice the habit of parking cars. One recalls that in earlier times in New York one never saw horses hitched in the main streets. That habit prevailed in the rural cities fifty years ago and was pleasant and highly convenient, but one does not recall the evidences of it half a century ago in the main thoroughfares of New York. But now the motor cars stand by the sidewalks not hitched but not occupied, and one wonders at the patience of a public that allows it and pays the cost of it.

As said, it is very expensive, this motor car detail of current American civilization. To be sure, the one cheap thing in New York is taxicabs. They are an immense luxury and convenience. The whole motor car innovation is a wonderful luxury, a wonderful convenience, otherwise we should not sacrifice to it as we do; but it is very expensive. The State of New York has voted a bond issue of three hundred million dollars to be spent in the abolition of grade crossings in the State. Of course, that means motor cars. Too many are smashed up at railroad crossings; too many people are killed. There must be many, many families in which the leading item in the cost of living is the car, and the other items are adjusted to what is left after item one is settled for. And there is more to be said for this arrangement than average mossbacks would suppose.

Don't you wonder where it is coming out? Don't you wonder where this phase of civilization of which the triumph of the motor car is so signally a detail is leading us all to? How far beyond calculation it all is!

Will something check the motor car,—the autogyro, maybe? Will relief of the roads come by invasion of the air, or shall we merely digest the automobile, expense and all, or become immune to it? Of course, we may do that, but the thought of it all is tiring. And, indeed, that is the fault of this changing world—it is too tiring. An ordered life is a great conservator of strength; and this disordered life that we now experience is a great consumer of it. "We shall try to live quietly," says a bride. (Another headline) Oh, yes, but shall we succeed?

If you live in a great city it tires you, or at least draws on your strength, merely to walk in the street. At every crossing you have to take notice not to be run over. We live indeed, wherever we are, practically on a railroad track. Country or town, that is much the same. If we cross the road it amounts to what used to be walking on the track, only it is much more perilous because more cars pass on it. To this condition of things one must pay attention; his mind must be on keeping alive when he goes out. If he crosses the street he must think of nothing else while he is about it. All that draws on strength, not unwholesomely if one has the strength to draw on, but incessantly. What is expected of the rising generation is not only that they shall have the strength to draw upon, but that they will develop an instinctive capacity to handle these things. Meanwhile, all old methods seem slow and the tendency is to drift toward speed in everything. Any one who lives in the country and is concerned with gardening or agriculture is likely to notice this tendency. A handy man on a farm nowadays will make a garden and run a car. His propensity will be, so far as noticed by this observer, to drift away from agriculture toward mechanics. Following a horse-drawn plow, weeding a garden, seem tedious exercises compared with driving a power mower or going on the road in a Ford. But the strain of plowing with a horse was less. The strain of weeding a garden was on the back but not much on the nerves. The society of horses and cows and pigs and chickens was as a rule more soothing than the society of motor cars and automatic engines. Nevertheless, we are not going back to the animals for society to the exclusion of our machines. Everything is more imaginable in the way of change than that we should forego water running in pipes and modern plumbing, or go back from motor cars and smooth roads to horse-drawn vehicles and mud. We may be on the road to destruction with all our mechanisms, but whatever road we are on we shall not turn back. We shall go through to the end of it and get to wherever it leads us.

BUT it is a curious journey. Consider crime! So rampant, so prevalent, so very bold. What does all that mean? We notice that these violent crimes are mostly done by very young men—with some assistance, at times, from young girls. They are amazing! How does it come that these young persons who do them are what they are, and can do what they do? How does it happen that our apparatus of order is so baffled by them; that they are able to get away with so many of these extraordinary crimes? As to what they *are*, what minds they have, there are all sorts of theories. They are the product of the Great War, which taught the use of firearms to four million men and made that knowledge so common and prevalent that it passed along down to the rising generation. The War, too, made killing common and diminished respect for human life. Do you remember the bayonet exercises that were taught to the infantry recruits? Naturally, crimes of violence in such extraordinary quantity as we have are related to war. Perhaps, too, they are related in moderation to the movies, but that is only to say that they come out of current life. The movies come out of current life, so does all the literature of the time; so does crime, and especially these crimes of violence. Somebody else will say that they are due to the decline of religion, and the Fundamentalists will lay them to Darwin. Drys will lay them to the Wets and to their disregard of law, and tell us that while we tolerate bootleggers we deserve to have our throats cut and our jewels stolen, and had better expect that. Wets will tell us that the reason why the gunmen operate uncaught is that the time and energy of the police in the United States are taken up trying to prevent the citizens of this country from getting a drink, and trying to keep motor cars moving in the streets. All these causes contribute to our crime records. A magistrate says that the education our schools give turns out boys who know how to play and can dress well, go to the movies, play with the girls and run motor cars, but do not know a trade and have no means of making a living. When these young men come out of school they feel the need of incomes to support their habits of life—and, not knowing how to earn the money, they get it as they can.

But of all the contributors to crime, the one that is most important seems to be the motor car. It is that, more than anything else, which has changed life. The head devil of all the innovators is Henry Ford. Shall we condemn him for that? By no means! We would not part with what he has accomplished even to get rid of some of its awful

consequences. If Henry is the dog, and the bootleggers and the gunmen, and the careless drivers
and the corrupted youths, and the general increase
of the perils of life, are the fleas, still we would
not kill the dog to get rid of the fleas. Henry is
just something that happened to us—like radium.
He personifies a considerable increase of fatalities,
but he also personifies an extraordinary detail of
what we think is Progress; of the mechanistic civilization, in which we live precariously, move with
caution but at increased speed, and have such being
as by exercise of vigilance we are able to conserve.

What is the outlook for farming? Apparently,
old-style farming is a dead duck, and agriculture
is to be saved by organization and machinery. Food
will have to be raised and undoubtedly will be
raised; some of it as a by-product of country living; the bulk of it by large-scale farming, co-
operative marketing, and such contrivances for
wholesale production and distribution. Pretty
much everything in this world that is not already
adjusted to mechanism must become so. Henry
Ford the other day blurted out a remonstrance
against the propensity to join everyone to some
organization. Master himself of one of the
greatest organizations in the country, he still was
all for having people think their own thoughts
and manage their own minds. That was curious,
but encouraging. With all his wonderful exploits
in mass production, he is still an individualist. What
he has done is the product of his own thoughts and

his own mind, and wonderful to say, he seems still to see the individual mind and the individual will, as primary forces and organization secondary and subject to them.

WELL, that helps to give one hope. All these matters that we have been talking about seem to have to do with the material part of life, but still they are all secondary matters. The primary things are those which concern the spirit of man, what it can see, what it can imagine, what it can aspire to, what it really wants. That is the idea that remains in the back of the mind of those persons, of whom Mr. Coolidge is one, who say that nothing can save the world except religion. That is true. When they say "religion," as a rule they use a word they cannot define. They don't know precisely what they want, but they know they want something, they feel the need of something, and they call that something religion.

For this life we are living does not seem to be a product of the Christian religion as it was understood one or two generations ago; it has come to pass without permission of our pastors and our preachers, come out of the increase of knowledge, and the vigor of the human mind, and is going its course as it must, with no particular concern for what is said in churches, nor for the Sermon on the Mount, nor even for the Ten Commandments. The main effort of the various churchmen has been to try to hobble it with legislation. They have given encouragement to the idea of making

conduct good by law; they have supported restrictions of various kinds, most conspicuously "Prohibition." Some of them struggle to regulate what
the schools shall teach, what plays shall be played,
what books shall be read. Most of that effort is
beside the mark. This extraordinary mechanistic
civilization is a kind of Samson that is not going
to be bound by green withs. It is partly good and
partly bad—but whatever else it is, it is full of
vigor, and is going down the middle of the road
considerably regardless of signs put up by the
politicians or the clergy. We cannot do much more
than watch it. The great trees of humanity will
bear their appointed fruits with very little regard
to our sentiments as to whether the fruits are
wholesome, or otherwise. What will come out of
the United States will depend upon what has been
put into the United States. What will come out
of Britain and France and Western Europe generally will depend upon what has been put into the
nations that occupy those parts. What will come
out of Russia will depend upon what Russia is—
and though she is new in a way, she wasn't made
yesterday. So, out of the East, will come what
the yellow people and the brown people have in
them, groups, no doubt colliding in times with
other groups; powers contending; powers co-
operating on an unprecedented scale for mutual
help and protection, but nobody and no combination of powers likely to be long successful in controlling the destinies of any considerable people
on this earth against their will.

Reopening Under New Management

N THE ANNUAL REPORT ISSUED LAST FALL by the President of Columbia University, a document of extraordinary interest and value, there occurs this passage:

As the years pass and the time comes when our older scholars of distinction and large achievement apply to be relieved of farther active service, they are uniformly asked where the University is to look for the best and most competent scholars for appointment to succeed those who are laying aside their burdens. With discouraging frequency the reply is made that there are no outstanding names which deserve special consideration, but that a choice must be made from a larger or a smaller group of mediocrities. When the question is pressed as to why such a condition exists, particularly in fields of knowledge that are eagerly pursued and that have large present public interest and importance, the answer is that while there are many narrow men of competence within the limitations of their interest, there are few broad men able to grasp and to interpret a given field of knowledge, as well as to advance its boundaries by independent study and reflection.

To very much the same purport is a bit of testimony derived from quite a different source, to wit: from a medium sitting in company, and communicating, or purporting to do so, the sentiments of invisibles to their friends still in this life. Attached to the name of a man well known in the great work of constructing northwestern railroads of the United States, and addressed to another

man well known to him in life and in the same
employment, came this:

> Does it ever occur to you that when our generation passes,
> something distinctly real in American life will be lost?   There
> are no such minds at work now as Hill or Kitson, Moffatt, and
> the rest, that came up in our neck of the woods; no one to take
> their place.   Instead of a few real people, a great mass is
> coming along and where is it all going to end?   That is what
> we (the invisibles) are thinking about.   That is what we are
> wondering.   Even to-day the laws are being flouted as never
> before.   This either means that the laws are bad, or that there
> is too little resistance and stamina to enforce laws.   Certainly
> something is wrong.

We have then the impression of the veterans of
teaching and of the veterans of certain lines of
material development, that their sort has done its
work and has gone, or is going, for good, and that
more of their kind are not to be expected, and
they wonder how the world is going to get along
without it; and neither living survivors nor communicating shades seem very hopeful about mankind confronting successfully so grave a failure of
what seems to them necessary energy and guidance.

All that is just another indication of the ending
of a period of time and the beginning of a new
one.   The management of the world is not going
to be such as it has been.   Roosevelt and Wilson
have passed on, and Coolidge is President.   The
managers in the new period are apparently to be
men of another sort than the men of the old, and
with other talents directed to other aims.

Of course, that is always happening but nowadays in an unusual degree.   When one wants to

know who is going to run the world that is making, he turns, of course, to youth, and never was youth more confident that it can do it than it is to-day. Never was it cockier, never more irreverent to the conclusions of its elders on all subjects, never more undaunted, more inquisitive, or bolder in inquiry and suggestion. Just at this writing a convention of college students gathered from all over the country has been meeting in Chicago to consider whether the church is up to its present job. The inquiry is timely enough, but think of its being undertaken by a lot of college boys!

THIS transference of the concerns of this life and this world to people of another sort from those who have managed it up to now means that the job itself has changed; that some things important to life are accomplished; that another set of things is to be undertaken. When Doctor Butler talks about "mediocrities," when the admonitory shade speaks of "a great mass" coming along, it cannot really mean degeneration of mind or spirit. It must mean rather the development of a new generation for a new kind of work, a work of limitation and adjustment, a work probably of more precision than the job of "Hill, Kitson, Moffatt," and the rest, a great work of providing that an immense number of people shall live together in the use and enjoyment of an enormous collection of material provisions, shall share somehow in the production and enjoyment of enormous wealth, shall give and take without

destructive fighting, shall have all the freedom
that is consistent with order, and more and more
of it as the provision of order is more wisely and
intelligently conducted. The past management of
the world, and especially the American world, has
been largely pioneering. It has called for courage,
energy, boldness of conception, and a driving power
of construction that at times have been ruthless.
The age that is now come calls for more scruples,
more skill, nicer calculation and, besides all that, it
seems evident that there is coming to it the exploration of extraordinary fields of new knowledge.
There is more for our new leaders and managers
than a nicer adjustment of what past leaders
have accomplished. They are going to have a field
of their own, and it may be by their achievement
in that field that their qualities and powers will
mainly be rated, though the job of adjustment
seems for the moment quite enough to engage
them.

The world is greatly oversupplied with rough-
neck legislation. The Treaty of Versailles made a
great contribution to it; American Prohibition did
the like. Laws and their administration in these
States are under constant discussion and are all but
universally censured. Europe, trying to adjust
its bellyful from Versailles, is doing a kind of egg
dance, trying to manage its necessary activities
without smashing anything. Authority of every
kind has. declined. The respect paid to money
has been waning for twenty-five years. The men
who can get it are no longer looked upon as wise

because of their demonstrated capacity to become rich. Creeds in the last generation found it hard to share the world of belief with science; but nowadays science is at least as much questioned as creeds have been. Hardly any of its conclusions nowadays are accepted as final. Nothing in science seems proof against the possibility that something discovered to-morrow may contradict it. Even the scientific method is assailed as not of universal application. As to that Doctor Butler said in his report above quoted: "The essential fact in all scientific study is the use and the comprehension of the scientific method. Nothing is to be taken for granted and no test, whether quantitative or qualitative, is to be overlooked. Every conclusion as it is reached is held subject to the results of verification, modification, or overthrow by later inquiry or by discovery of new methods and processes of research." Furthermore he said, "One would suppose that after a half-century of this experience and this discipline, the popular mind would bear some traces of the influence of scientific method, and that it would be guided by that method, at least in part, in reaching results and in formulating policies in social and political life." For himself, however, he could find no evidence of such an effect. Passion, prejudice, and unreason, he says, sway men just as if the scientific method had never been heard of and, in searching for a reason for this, he concludes that science has not been and is not being well taught and, since that belongs to his employment as college president, he goes on to discuss it.

It may be permitted to wonder whether as yet the scientific method can cover religion. The great beliefs which have moved the minds of men and affected their action have come by faith, by belief not based on scientific proof but somehow attained without it. If we look forward to a world governed by what we are used to call knowledge we must despair because of the great disparity between the size of the job and the means of passing around knowledge enough to handle it. That is why most of the thoughtful people, when they think about human life on this earth and its complicated prospects, say that the only thing that can pull us through is religion. If we have enough religion we can manage with a moderate amount of knowledge. Knowledge means experts. We do not have to have so very many of them. We do have to have the will to use them, and that will religion may supply.

THE man who knows is helpless without a power somewhere which permits his knowledge to be used. Regard the coal situation which, at this writing, shows no prospect of solution. But it could be solved; anyone would admit that. It would not be difficult to supply the necessary knowledge and sympathy and integrity to reach a solution fair for the time being to miners, operators, and consumers, and to embody in that solution a provision for self-correction as conditions change. That could be done if the minds of the parties most concerned could meet. Very likely that will be the solution, but at this writing no one can say when. It is the same way with the world generally. Life can be planned so as to move along prosperously if only the people concerned can be induced to agree to the plan.

Someone said the other day that all the frontiers in Europe were unjust; that is to say, unjust to some people. It seems obviously true that the frontiers in Europe have got to diminish in economic significance before the enjoyment of life in Europe can be what it is physically possible to make it. That continent, as we see it, and as more and more Europeans see it, ought to be some kind of a United States. This may be coming, and this mass of young experts that is going to manage the world may somehow get it done.

The great value of the young is that they have less to unlearn than the older people. Where there is to be a large conveyance of respected properties to the junk pile, it is the young who are suitable to be called to the work. The fathers of our Republic were most of them pretty young, Hamilton particularly; though Hamilton, it is true, was by no means a radical, but a convinced conservative, who believed in government by aristocracy, distrusted and despised control by popular majorities, and only accepted the Constitution because some sort of machinery of administration was indispensable and the Constitution was the best that offered. Hamilton was not disposed to throw on the junk pile anything he could keep. He was at heart a monarchist, but with him it was a case of any port in a storm and, so feeling, he was a useful pilot to democracy. But Napoleon, who junked so much of Europe a century ago, was also young. The junking of our world has been pretty well accomplished by the War, but whereas the older generation may know something about putting it together as it was, the younger generation may prove to be more efficient in putting it together as it ought to be.

THE processes of change are most interesting to watch. For example, the foreign debts that are owed to us. What is really going on about those debts is a gradual readjustment of the American mind. Little by little, we are thinking of them differently. One day we read that France is immensely prosperous and can pay everything it owes us, and the next day we read that it is a superhuman job to keep the franc from going to grass; that the best people in France are taxed to destitution; that her budget does not balance and that she cannot make it balance. We get a like order of stories about England: that England is going downhill; has lost half her trade; is choked up with unemployed, and ought not to be paying us anything. The last may be true— true for the time being anyway. The rest of it describes, no doubt, a temporary condition which will presently be better. But nothing that has been done about those debts is more than provisional. It is like the discoveries and conclusions of science, useful to-day, to-morrow, and probably the rest of the week, but likely any moment to be superseded by new knowledge. Our world is run on working hypotheses—that is the best we can do and that is all which has been done about the foreign debts.

That, however, has been very useful, and really we have done much better by Europe than we get credit for either from Europe or from many of ourselves. Anyone who wants to think so may be assisted to that opinion by the address of Secretary Kellogg before the Council on Foreign Relations on December 14th in New York, while the present attitude of the Administration was doubtless imparted by Secretary Mellon, when, on January 4th, in arguing before the Ways and Means Committee of the House for acceptance of the agreement negotiated with Italy, he said:—"*The entire foreign debt is not worth as much to the American people in dollars and cents as a prosperous Europe as customer.*" That is the pith of the situation about those debts. Those words of Scripture, "Let the dead bury their dead," have application sometimes to money matters. The first thought of the living must be, not for yesterday, but for to-morrow.

The problem of the foreign debts seems to be on the way toward solution, and the spirit and the pact of Locarno have encouraged everyone about Europe, and the coal strike will probably be settled before these lines are read, and the hands of the younger generation are reaching for the steering wheel of the car humanity now rides in, and the feet of men still young will presently step on the gas. Timorous passengers are welcome to alight if they prefer and can find a suitable getting-off place not in the earthquake belt and not liable to floods. But it is much more interesting to stay in the car and see where it gets to.

There are those whose chosen field is that of knowledge who expect great things from the new drivers. Professor Bovie of Harvard was quoted as saying in a Lowell Institute lecture early in January that man "is just now undergoing an evolutionary change at a more rapid rate than has ever been experienced before. Surely formed in God's image, he shares in the bringing into existence of a new kind of individual, and we may expect achievements from the social organism beyond the power of the imagination to conceive."

That is the sort of talk the really hopeful observers give us. Let us stay on with them at least until it becomes less awkward to get out.

Immortality as a World-Cure

MAY 1926

F SOME FULLY INFORMED AND COMPETENT person could put his finger on the pulse of this world and tell us how it is, the information would be welcomed in many quarters. One does not necessarily notice it as he walks abroad, but it is a fact that doubt exists in considerable quantity whether human life just now is progressing toward better conditions or worse ones. It is moving, and the impression is very general that we are at the beginning of a new age. Belief abounds abundantly that once this new age gets well a-going it will be a better age than the world has so far had, but the rub, the worry, is over the interval between these presents and such time as the new age gets well started.

There is a horrid suspicion, and quite well diffused, that the present population of this world has not got average sense enough to be used just as it is in peopling the new age, and that it may be necessary to get rid of quite a bit of it. It must be the consideration of that necessity which makes people anxious. There is apt to be a clean-up before any great terrene change. To be sure we had the War, and that should have been clean-up enough for all purposes. But was it? Doubts about that make stockbrokers wonder where their customers should alight, make American politicians uncertain how long Mr. Coolidge is going to last in Washington, make builders consider whether the business current they count on is trustworthy or will lag and leave them with empty buildings on their hands. "To-day," said Bishop Slattery to the Congregational Club of Boston, "there is the possibility of a great catastrophe, and I am not altogether doubtful that it may be growing now," and he went on to say that what with the current discontents and hatreds and anti-Christian propaganda, all sorts of Christian churches might have to get together to save the Christian Church from wreck.

Conan Doyle and many others have had from spiritist sources these same suggestions of impending catastrophe. They are common in spiritist books. They are also put out with confidence and precision by the British-Israel people—those who connect the Anglo-Saxons with the Lost Tribes, and know to a day when hell-to-pay will begin and when it will end. Folks who go into particulars about it say we shall have very interesting expositions of the effect of poison gas on large cities. On the other hand, another intimation attributed to the spirit world says that there is a big war on already, but they call it a bloodless war, a war between spirituality and materialism. That, at least, is so; at least one can feel that conflict going on and, if anyone says it has always been going on, the answer is that it is going on now much more palpably than usual.

PEOPLE who know a little something, and have come to know anything unusual, as a rule do not tell it all. They cannot. No one would believe them. You can put across to another mind only so much as that other mind is prepared to receive. Of course, receptive capacity in minds may increase greatly, and what one cannot take in at one time he may see the point of later. One notices that in rereading books. Books that meant one thing to us when we were young usually mean something quite different if we reread them when we come to maturity. Really, we do not stay about in this world for nothing; almost all of us get something, and a good many get a good deal. If you are discouraged about yourself and do not think you have made due progress, go find some fairly good book that you read in childhood or in youth, and see what it says to you now. But, as was being said, if by any chance someone knows something out of the common he cannot impart it successfully except to persons who know enough to take it in.

That may be one reason why the Corporation of Harvard College picks the kind of speakers it does to give the Ingersoll lecture. Not everybody knows what the Ingersoll lecture is, but it is one of the humble facts of current life, and now and then it gets a little advertisement. Miss Caroline Ingersoll, of Keene, N. H., who died in 1893, left five thousand dollars to Harvard University to make good a wish of her father and establish a lectureship on The Immortality of Man, one lecture to

be given every year (if convenient) and the lecturer paid and his discourse printed out of the
income of the fund. It is thirty-three years since
the lectureship was founded and in that time there
have been eighteen Ingersoll lectures on the immortality of man, and the larger part of them delivered by persons who either did not approve of
immortality as a prospect for man or did not see it
coming to him. The lecturers have included Dr.
George A. Gordon, William James, Benjamin Ide
Wheeler, Josiah Royce, John Fiske, and William
Osler; and the lecture delivered in 1922 was by
Dr. Kirsopp Lake, Harvard Professor of Ecclesiastical History, who admitted that he does not think
personality survives or ought to. In all this series
of expositions no one has yet been called upon—
so far as appears—who was a master of the
goings-on now cropping out on all sides on which
are based the claims of the spiritists that the survival of death by personality is a demonstrated
fact. These persons are now the most active partisans of the immortality of man. They have the
most confident theory about it and their theory is
supported by the best stories. Some of them are
scientists of great distinction; others of them are
writers well known and well approved. It may be
that the reason why the Harvard Corporation has
never picked one of these highly eligible people for
this job has been that, looking about in its home
community, it could not see a sufficient proportion
of minds who would be able to take in what a
spiritist lecturer, really informed about man's im-

mortality, would be able to tell them. Or it may
be that the Corporation knows nothing about current spiritism and supposes it to be mere diversion
of the feeble-minded. If so, so much the more may
one suggest that it is time the Ingersoll lecture
was given by some real expert in current knowledge of the subject it was intended to explore.

How much would it benefit the world to
have confidence in immortality much more
positive? Doctor Lake said in his lecture that
when confidence in the future life was more
general and vivid too many people put in too
much of their time trying to save their souls, and
the great human errand of keeping body and soul
together was over much neglected. We are strong
nowadays in all that pertains to the maintenance
of the body. Our wise men have checked diseases;
they make physical repairs very skilfully; they
furnish shelter and clothing no end; they feed us
more liberally and with greater variety than the
mass of people was ever fed before. They help us
in our migrations. In all temporal concerns our
world goes strong, but whether soul and body are
successfully kept together is still something of a
question. The body gets more attention than the
soul. The body, which sometimes has been valued
chiefly because it was the soul's habitation, is in
danger nowadays of being valued purely for itself.

And that is not a good thing. The body is altogether too transitory to carry the main part of

one's investments. It is important of course; health
is important, immensely so, but even health is
more important from its relation with the soul.
The soul needs a healthy body to live in. At
least we think so now. In the Middle Ages, when
belief in the after life was a good deal more vivid
than it is at present, it was considered that to plague
the body was profitable to the soul. Not so nowadays. We think we do much better when our bodies
are healthy and clean than otherwise. We are
advanced enough for that: we think of them as
habitations, as instruments, and pay due attention
to them as good housekeepers should. One does not
see the danger that Doctor Lake spoke of; that of
neglecting temporal things in order to save our
souls. On the contrary, the current theory of life
and conduct is that by the proper discharge of
temporal duties we advance spiritually and fit ourselves for further activities and advancement in
the *au de là*. That is one change that has come to
religion as we Western people look at it. Whereas
in older times it was more concentrated on self-
denial and self-abasement, now its errand seems
largely to be to make a better habitation of this
world and better physical people of its inhabitants.

But neither of these ends is likely to be attained
by putting it first. They are secondary ends and
cannot survive and prosper unless the great primary end gets due and constant attention. The
spiritual part of life is the substance; the temporal
part is the reflection of it. Turn it the other way

around and it does not work. The spirit is the master of the body. If one is in a state of spiritual health he is in a condition highly conducive to physical health. That is much more nearly true than to say if he is in a state of physical health he is necessarily in a condition conducive to spiritual health, for one may be very healthy physically and bad spiritually, and he may be very unhealthy physically for some reason, and still pretty good spiritually. But still it remains that, of the two states, the state of spiritual health is more important than the other, and more conducive to every sort of well being.

To everything spiritual, to religion especially, the theory of immortality is of the first importance. St. Paul described it as the very pith of religion. So it is and, of course, it is the pith of all psychical knowledge. That it is important hardly anyone denies. The people who do not yet believe in it make the best case they can for life without it and, of course, in that they do well, but the case they make is not any too satisfactory. Doctors nowadays practice pretty generally to bring about in so far as they can a good spiritual condition in their patients. In many cases that is of the first importance, but the great patient of all the doctors in these days is this world that we live in, generally admitted to be pretty sick, admitted also to be important to its inhabitants, and admitted more and more generally to be incurable in the long run by any but spiritual means. Physical means are comparatively easy. They will be tried and are being tried.

So it was in times past. They were tried and tried again, and about the best that can be said for them is that our world survived them. But in the years to come, so great has been man's progress on the material side that the prospect is that the present civilization in our world will not survive the medication by material means which is war. That is why the search for light on spiritual power is so lively in these times.

IF THIS world is related to the world invisible, the advantages and also the limitations of that relation need to be better defined than they are now. We should know what we can get to advantage out of the invisible, and what we need not try for because it is not for us. That this world is related to a world invisible has been a detail of belief for thousands of years, and is dutifully admitted by every church steeple which points to the sky. If we accept that belief we are entitled to do what we can about it. If we reject it we can save some money on steeples which is, to be sure, the present disposition, especially in cities where commercial and residential buildings run up to great heights and steeples are obstructed as well as comparatively unprofitable as producers of revenue.

Suppose we got to estimate people more as souls and not so much as industrial possibilities or financial entities, would that be good for us? When you sit in the street car and look at the people—look at their bodies, their faces, which is what you see—do you think of what is inside of them, or merely of what is outside? If you think of the life within, that is, of their souls, and examine their exteriors for indication that their souls are in a good case or not, they all become interesting. There is something rather awful about the current disposition to think of human beings as consumers, as producers, as accumulators of money to put into savings banks, as possible buyers of everything imaginable, as creators and diffusors of wealth. All these aspects of human beings are important, but whoever sees them as souls sees more of them than can be discerned by contemplation of all their temporal functions.

Another thing—much of what we have been taught, and have thought, to be good, is not good; is merely goody-good, or bad. Much of what we have been taught, and have thought, to be bad, is not bad; quite a bit of it is even good. What is convenient and disturbing to the *status quo* is usually put down as bad, but in all civilizations the estimates of what is good and what is bad have been very faulty, and ours is no exception. To correct its ideals and persuade people that in divers particulars they have seen crooked, is a fairly rough job, but it is important, and in these times it is proceeding quite effectively.

Revolt

JULY 1926

OUNG PUBLIUS SAYS THE TIMES ARE FULL of revolt. He says that people who do not see it should have their eyes tested; that people who do not feel it should see if their knee action is all right; for he considers that it is something one cannot afford not to see, not to feel, not to consider as to its causes, the power of it, and its destination. All along the line he sees the same kind of commotion, a revolt against the same general enemy with all sorts of differences in particulars. As he sees it, it is a revolt against usurpation of authority, against old rules that have lost their reasonableness, against new rules that never had reasonableness, against exaction of fidelity to creeds or customs in details in which they have ceased to express to modern minds what once they did express. It is a revolt against outworn forms and against the ambitions of new regulators; in a way a revolt against authority, but not all authority; rather against tyranny; against authority that has not due warrant—authority that does not keep order but instigates disorder. The real strength of the current revolt against Prohibition lies back, so Publius says, of all questions about the good or bad of alcohol. The strength of it is in the deep sentiment of people who are not unduly concerned about what they shall drink or not drink, but who are more afraid of excessive regulation than they are of rum. They see that some abridgement of the right to go on one's own way is necessary, is reasonable. They do not object to that. They object to what is not necessary, what is unreasonable, what is impertinent, what is fanatic; and they object for a reason no less deep than that resistance in such a case is the price of liberty, and that liberty, misuse the word as you will, is necessary to human progress. Young Publius assures us that all the old slogans are coming out in these days from their places of deposit and re-establishing themselves in the voices of men; that one hears again: Eternal vigilance is the price of liberty, and Who would be free, themselves must strike the blow; that it is remarkably a revolt against compulsion, running up and down through society, crossing the seas, skipping all barriers, compassing the world.

So big as that! Well, what is it? What does it make for? For war? For revolution? For world peace?

Provided that the revolt is real and not merely imagined, it might make for all three—for war, for revolution, for world peace, each in its turn. But we have had plenty of war and much prefer not to expect any more, and confidence in war and revolution as precursors to world peace has been seriously impaired by the record of the last six years. At least we like to think that if war and revolution are necessary steps to world peace, they are steps which have been taken, and that we have not got to go through them all again. Let us think then of

revolt, as above reported, as a finishing process and
not as part of an original smash that is necessary before the properties of civilization can be re-assembled. They are being re-assembled now. One can
pretty well see that, even though he sees revolt a-
plenty at the same time.

Is the world safe as it stands? Not by a jugful,
and that one may say without any thought of Prohibition. Does it look to be safe as it is? Do we
think it can go on as it is? It does not look safe,
and most of us think it can hardly go on as it is, but
we think it is bound to improve and is improving
now; but it improves or at least changes with such
curious differences. Some of the nations run off
toward concentrated authority, Italy and Spain
especially, and one may say Russia as well, but in
England and here the propensity is the other way.

The disturbance considerably concerns religion.
Why is the Mexican government turning out
foreign-born priests? Is it because it favors authority, or opposes it? Doubtless it favors authority for
itself but not for a rival. A number of governments now look askance at priests and ministers of
religion. The Soviets do. So do many observers in
these States look askance at the embattled clergy of
the Methodists.

Is it part of the revolt in the world to scrutinize
the clergy and speculate as to whether or not they
are useful? It is proper enough to scrutinize them,
to observe, to measure, and reflect about them. It
is done a great deal just now in this country, not
with fear, not with anger, but merely in a spirit of

inquiry. The churches are doing very well so far as their incomes and their memberships go. They never raised more money or had any better increase of membership than last year, but it is true enough that they are being carefully inspected.

A clergyman, Doctor Empringham, the Secretary of a Church Temperance Society, told a group of New Jersey Republicans the other day that the churches had forsaken the fundamental principle of Christianity in forcing sumptuary laws on the American people and were no longer entitled to exemption from taxation. He said they were relieved of taxation because it was thought that they helped to keep order, and so to save money for police. Nowadays, Doctor Empringham said, they are promoting disorder, and putting the courts and the police to expense. That is a novel idea and is worth considering, and likely to be considered by many people who want the Church to be worth its keep and if it isn't, want to know it.

THROUGH all the current unrest seems to run this idea that many things now regulated by laws and rules would take better care of themselves if let alone. That is not, to be sure, a new idea. A poet who had understanding of spiritual things was conscious of it when he wrote:

> Serene will be our days and bright
> And happy will our nature be,
> When love is an unerring light,
> And joy its own security.

Wordsworth's times were not so very different from

ours. They included great wars just as ours do; great changes in society; questionings of everything. Wordsworth approved of love and joy as guides to life, but he did not trust them implicitly. Clinging to both, the rock he found necessary as the basis of conduct was Duty.

In the *Hibbert Journal* for April there is a story, appropriate to these times, of the efforts of a philosopher to reform a state. The story has been extracted by Mr. Post, of Haverford College, from the Letters of Plato, for Plato was the reformatory philosopher. He had ideas about the Ideal State, and expected in his youth to go into politics to try to realize them. But two revolutions happened in Athens and upset things so, and made them so much worse than they were before, that Plato saw no chance there for his political ideas to gain headway. So he turned back to philosophy and stayed on the pursuit of it until in due course of time, acquiring great reputation, he was invited to come to Syracuse and give instruction to Dionysius, the young despot of Sicily and Italy, who seemed in need of expert advice. So along went Plato to Syracuse and as to what he found there his words are:

"I found myself utterly at odds with the sort of life that is there termed a happy one, a life taken up with Italian and Syracusan banquets, an existence that consists in filling oneself up twice a day, never sleeping alone at night, and indulging in all the practices attendant on that way of living. In such an environment no man under heaven, brought up in self-indulgence, could ever grow to be wise.

So marvellous a temperament as that is not in nature."

Dionysius liked the life so described. Plato lectured to him until the despot got tired and shipped him off to Ægina to be sold as a slave. The main result of his visit was the conversion of one pupil, Dion, who, being an able young man and thoroughly penetrated with Plato's puritan principles, stayed sober, lived continently, and came to high place in the government under Dionysius. When that tyrant died and his young son succeeded him, Dion came to be for a while the real power in government in Sicily. Forthwith he sent for Plato to come and help make good his early ideals. Plato was received with great enthusiasm in Syracuse. For a while his mission went admirably. The gin palaces were closed and the addiction to philosophy and mathematics went very strong. But it did not last. The old life was more popular. Presently Dion was set adrift in a boat, and though there is more to this story, the upshot of it all was that Plato fell down hard as a political reformer and Dion with him.

Always the Puritans fall down when they try to make Puritanism compulsory. Always the Christians fall down when they try to make Christianity compulsory. Rules about belief enforced by penalties—what good are they? What good have they ever been? "Creeds," says a writer in the May *Atlantic*, "are the prison of faith and the symbols of death," and the same writer quotes Charles Buller (friend of Thackeray) as crying, "For heaven's sake do not destroy the Established Church. It is the only thing that stands between us and Christianity."

Some things can be done by rules, some things by laws, but not much more than may be the expression of such knowledge of life as the mass of the people affected have arrived at. The Common Law was such an expression. It always stood for the civilization of its day, and as civilization advanced, it advanced with it. But statutes or word-made laws of any kind that at most express the opinion of part of the people as to what is good for all of the people, are of limited benefit. If they last long enough and show benefits enough to establish their standing by common consent, they help matters; otherwise they go to the scrap heap.

How Comes Understanding?

WHO HAS UNDERSTANDING AND HOW DOES he get it? Is it solely a product of learning or of other and more intuitive processes besides? Consider Dean Inge. Very able, a scholar; his mind crammed with knowledge and history and able to gather more from contemporary documents. But has he in a high degree understanding? One would be sorry to think so, so very downcast are his feelings about the future of civilization and especially of England. Compare him with Henry Ford. One of the magazines that tells about country houses had pictures the other day of Henry Ford's home outside of Detroit, and there was a library in it with shelves full of books. But Henry has never prided himself on his knowledge of what was in books and though, of course, he must know even of them much more than is supposed, his great forte is not book knowledge but that insight into certain phases of human affairs which is the result of experiment, observation, and reflection. Henry's great asset is not so much his knowledge as his imagination. It is probable—indeed, it is almost obvious, that in understanding of human life and of its errand in this world Henry Ford is very much the superior of Dean Inge. But then the difference between them is the difference between a genius and a scholar. What the scholar has, he has learned; what the genius gets, comes to him. He does not learn it, he sees it—becomes aware of it.

The spiritists have been taking notice that this year is the hundredth anniversary of the birth of Andrew Jackson Davis, called the Poughkeepsie Seer. His works, of which there are fifteen or twenty volumes, have been republished in Los Angeles. The substance of them has been put into a book in England, which is sold in New York bookstores. Conan Doyle calls him the Prophet of Spiritualism, and has a chapter about him in his new history of that activity. Davis emerged from obscurity in Poughkeepsie along about 1845. He was the son of a shoemaker, grew up with no more than the bare rudiments of education; at eighteen could read and write and not much more, but was found to possess clairvoyant and healing faculties, and was taken into hand by good people who got interested in him and helped in the development of his extraordinary faculties. With that much help he blossomed out shortly as a lecturer and author, starting with a book called *The Harmonial Philosophy*, published about 1847, which had in its day a very considerable circulation and evoked astonishment and high praise from such literary critics of that day as N. P. Willis, George Ripley, Parke Godwin, and Thomas Lake Harris. It was made up of discourses communicated apparently in a state of trance and was a philosophical work which expounded everything, explained most things, and forecast a good deal. It abounded in technical knowledge of various sorts which Davis could not possibly have acquired by ordinary means. Swedenborg, when he took up with the invisible world, already had a fair title to be called the most learned man in Europe; but this black-haired Davis had never learned anything, and how he produced this book and the succession of those that followed is a question for anyone who thinks he can answer it. Among other things, he predicted the motor car and the airplane with a curious prevision of details and of what must happen in mechanics before they could be. He finally brought up in Boston where he practiced healing for a long time and died at the age of eighty-four in 1910. His books seem to have been accepted as his. No fraud was brought home to him. His character was good. He was remarkably free from venality. He lived and died poor.

How did he do it? The natural inference that could be made from Davis and others like him is that knowledge is sometimes, perhaps oftentimes, communicated by processes other than study.

And as for understanding, one hardly gets it by study, though study commonly contributes to it. He learns what other persons have known, but to this knowledge he puts something of his own. His knowledge in a way is the collection of materials and tools that his imagination works with, and if he is oversupplied with such acquired knowledge his imagination may be stifled. Shakespeare seemed to know more than he had any visible means of learning. To be sure, he read some books—there were not so many in his time—but they account scantily for what he knew. The prospect improves, however, that when we know more than we do now we shall understand better the source from which Shakespeare got the information that he used. Christ in the Temple disputing with the doctors was not a prize scholar, though incredibly proficient for his age. His knowledge came some other way. Probably most people who show notable talent have a good deal given them that they never learned. Just now the world seems to need leaders. We cannot see where they are coming from, but there is faith that they will come; that men will turn up, or maybe women, who know more than they could have learned; who have the necessary gumption and devotion to pull the world right. For that arduous employment which has periodically to be undertaken, very curious people have sometimes been selected, and usually, though not always, persons not in favor with orthodox opinion, the reason being that the ailments of life usually spring from fixed policies of one sort or another, which have to be broken before there can be a cure. Minds that are set have to move. The orthodox and the upholders of the *status quo* resist movement, and somebody from the outside has to accomplish it over their heads. The Bible, Old Testament and New, is full of the triumphs of the outsiders over the orthodox, which may be one reason why it is so popular. The prophets seldom ran with the machine. They were usually out to break it, and often incurred the perils and inconvenience incident to that purpose.

Young Publius Is Disgruntled

OUNG PUBLIUS, WHOM I SPEAK OF SOME-
times, comes often to our house, talks freely
and always puts over on us complaints or
indictments of this or that detail of life as we now
see it lived. Publius has his meals regularly and
has no special trouble with them when eaten. He
seems to get a little to drink, has good health, a very
nice family, a good job, and terrestrial prospects of
reasonable felicity—unaffected by all of which good
fortune, he comes to our house with these diatribes
about the details of the *status quo.*

For example, I wish you could hear him talk
about the Hall trial. No one living in that wholesome fear of libel suits that stays the disclosures of
some intemperate minds would dare tell the whole
of what Publius says about that case; of why it
was got up; of what newspaper instigation this
recent trial had and why; of how intolerable an out-
rage it was on the family concerned, and so on and
so on. Anyone who reprinted all of his remarks
would be in danger of the grand jury at least; but
they were interesting to anyone sufficiently ignorant
to think they might be true, or sufficiently informed
to know they *were* true.

Publius is a lawyer, and he thinks that the bulk
of what little is now known about the management

of human affairs and the relations of visible to invisible life is known by the members of that profession. He thinks the available information of the
ministers is far, far behind what they need in their
business. He thinks rather better of doctors, for
the reason, perhaps, that he knows less about
medicine than he thinks he knows about religion.
He is willing to help in the support of doctors for
the sake of what they can do for his family. He
tries to keep up with the scientists and, indeed, does
keep along with them pretty well, but finds the limit
of their attainments too soon reached. When he
thinks they begin to guess he begins to grumble and
to say that, after all, they don't know much more
than the ministers.

Of course young Publius is safe enough in all
these aspersions of contemporary wisdom. It is
nothing new to find limits to the wisdom of the wise
and defects in its conclusions. But that disposition,
when geared to some knowledge and some intelligence, is particularly noteworthy and perhaps useful in these times when everything seems to be in
such a state of flux. Our river of life seems just
now to be running through a narrow cañon full of
rocks and tumult in which the rafts and boats which
we have launched are shaken and whirled about in a
way to make us wonder how many of them will
still be afloat when our river comes to smooth going
again. It is this hurrying passage that I like to
hear Publius discuss, because it really is a great
matter for discussion. I asked him the other night
if he wanted to cancel the foreign debts and had he

read Mr. Glasgow's discourse on that subject in the front pages of the December *Harper's.* He had not read it but would, and said that he was willing to cancel the debts if he could make the speech accompanying the cancellation. He seems to have something on his mind about Europe and about war which he wants to set free in such a manner that it will reach the listening ears of mankind. Well, one can guess what it is. Probably he has it in him to say that mankind is so stupid it deserves to have wars go on, and that Europe is so stupid she ought to pay the debts—which is, of course, true enough in a way, and if Publius felt that it was worth a few billion dollars to have it brought to notice as he could bring it, why, one sympathizes with his feeling.

WHAT our poor world needs is to be laughed at. Rabelais laughed at the Middle Ages, and is a best-seller to-day. Cervantes laughted at chivalry and still lives. Voltaire laughed at Church and State in prerevolutionary France, and is on the way to sit with the saints. One of the great cures for disorder is to laugh. If young Publius could make Europe see itself ridiculous in having its debts canceled, and could make us all see ourselves ridiculous for not being able to escape from war, it might be worth all that money. As for that special article in the December HARPER'S, to laugh at that is perhaps the most helpful way to take it. The question about those debts is what is best to do; not what is legal, not entirely what is possible, not what is the utmost money that can be squeezed out of Europe, but how much, if any, it will pay to take: what arrangement will in the long run be best for all hands. The American case is good enough at law, even at international law. When we got into the War we were needed in it. When our friends the Allies borrowed money of us they needed the money. When we began to lend it in quantity we said, this may be all we can do in this War, so we did it lavishly. But then we went on and spent vast sums on our own account, training troops and all that, and in the end were actually useful in the field.

We have title enough to receive what Europe can pay, but that does not get us anywhere, unless it is really profitable to have Europe pay us. That is the great question: whether it is good for the world, for mankind, for the human race that we should collect those debts in the modified degree which has now been negotiated. For we are part of the world, of the human race, of mankind, and we believe and not without due basis that we have come to be an important part. They tell us so, and we think so. This is considerably our world. The economists say that we have contrived, or it has happened to us, to have a third of its wealth in our possession. All that wealth is more valuable to us if the other two-thirds are also valuable. If they shrink unduly, our third will also shrink. If by tipping out those debts we can make the rest of our world more prosperous, it may be an excellent thing to do.

Almost anybody will admit as much as that. But
we are more or less embarrassed by being tied to
an ancient sentiment greatly respected in ordinary
affairs—that honest debts must be paid if the credit
of the debtors is to be sustained. Perhaps, however, in the great flux of things we shall presently
get back more generally to a view of certain forms
of property rights as something less permanent than
we have regarded them. A very large share of our
property rights consists nowadays of certificates of
indebtedness of one kind or another. To call all
debts off every fifty years, as the ancient Jews did,
would disturb our system a good deal and it is not
likely to be done. But the idea at the bottom
of it that the less lucky or less able should be
freed at stated periods from the domination of the
more fortunate and shrewder has plenty to be said
in support of it, and is indeed embodied in current
bankruptcy laws. That idea has an application to
the foreign debts. Countries must not be crushed;
nor driven into bankruptcy if it can be avoided.
Peoples must not be overburdened, standards of
living must not be kept too low indefinitely by national debts. That is not for the good of mankind
and does not pay. Nature, even political nature,
seems to work against it. In any country, in any
empire, where too large a share of the wealth gets
into too few hands, revolution begins to breed and
presently there is a new distribution. So of nations.
If they get too rich in comparison with their neighbors, presently they blow up.

MAYBE Publius will put forth some of these thoughts when he makes the address on the cancellation of debts, but very possibly he has better ones of his own. Another matter that concerns him is about the Church and marriage. We have had that amusing rumpus over the nullification by the authorities of the Vatican at Rome of a marriage which affected an American and an English family. It made the Protestant clergy in both those countries quite indignant. As for the laity, they have not shown temper about it, but have merely grinned. Publius is sure the Church has nothing to do with marriage anyhow. But then he is pretty young, and I never feel that he has yet reached final opinions about anything. The Church is almost universally of the opinion that people who marry should stay married. A great many of them do, and for manifold reasons it is a good plan; but the Church inclines to keep them married by making it hard for them to get loose from that condition. But nowadays efforts of the Church in that direction are largely defeated by secular law which lets people get divorce for a variety of reasons. Publius affects to think that the whole control by churches of marriage is a usurpation, and that they really have slight concern with it. If they held that church marriages made here remained in force in the life to come, that would be important. But they do not go so far as that. The most they hold is that a church marriage is good till death of one of the parties to it.

It seems to be with marriage a good deal as it is

with drink. If the rules are too strict you get a lot of bootleggers. Where the Church has been stricter than human nature has been inclined to endure, the bootlegging has been assisted by statute, and the secular courts have tried to make the rules match existing public sentiment. Perhaps the Church people after a while will get a divorce amendment into the Constitution. They show a disposition in that direction, but until we have digested Amendment 18, the adventure about divorce is not likely to succeed. We are going through a process of instruction about the possibility of making character by compulsion, or at least by compelling deportment whether there is character to back it or not. That is what our brethren tried to do who put over the Prohibition laws. It was possible to regulate the sale of rum. That had long been done. Their effort to do it differently was legitimate enough, but they went farther than that and tried to contrive to eliminate drinking by law. After six years of experiment it seems to be pretty well demonstrated that this cannot be done, and most of us expect to see the present laws either modified by legislation or nullified in a way by failure of enforcement. What the Church has tried to do about marriage is something of the same sort. With a sound and admirable ideal of marriage in its mind, it has tried always to impose it on human creatures who had not character enough to make it go. Once it could punish them if they were disobedient to its ordinances; now it can do no more than exclude them from church privileges.

Well, that seems proper enough if they wish to do it. It weighs a great deal with some people. Does anybody who faces marriage read up the laws of his State on that subject? Very few. For anybody but a lawyer it would be a difficult job of research. But does anyone read the Church service? Oh, yes, a great many people. The Church's influence in the direction of durable marriage is all to the good, but it is evident that it cannot compel anyone to remain married whose own conscience does not demand it, except, indeed, its own officers who may be deprived of their employment if they disobey. But though the Church's ideal of marriage is respected, its position on divorce is very widely questioned. It would hold together people who do not wish to stay married and as to whom there is no compelling reason why they should. The Church (all the churches) is considerably committed to the perpetuation of marriages which ought not to be perpetuated. That is the weak part of its position. The strong part of it is that it has the right ideal and does its best to promote its acceptance.

HEAVEN knows where it will come out in this matter. When the divorce lawyers of the Catholic Church in Rome nullified a marriage done with great formality by a Bishop of the Episcopal Church in the United States there was a general chuckle. The Protestant clergy was indignant, and said the Pope had no business to permit such a thing, and the Catholic clergy defended the action of the Rota, said it was all right and scolded the protesting Protestants. As for young Publius, he said the Pope had got in bad and the Rota's decision would make him trouble. But anyhow it was a very interesting case and world-wide discussion of it may in the end be helpful to an understanding of what in our present troubled and changeful times the relation of the Church to marriage really is and ought to be. The truth is, and it is no news, that we cannot rely on any organization to make us good or keep us good. When Charlie Chaplin's wife flounces out to consider whether she shall sue Charlie for one million or two million dollars, that is an illustration of what may happen to marriage when the Church has nothing to do with it. When the Rota nullified the Marlborough-Vanderbilt adventure, that illustrated what may happen when various churches have done all they could.

But it has all made people laugh and that, as said, is useful. Man-made laws have never been entirely right and never will be. They are the defective products of defective powers; milestones set up in the road of human progress. The expectation is that travelers will pass them, and happily they do, else were our earthly journey more disgruntling than it is. When you put wrong definitions of conduct into a constitution or a creed, it is like a wall across our path. We have to get over it somehow and in time we do.

Sun Spots and Politics

MARCH 1927

HILE THE FUNDAMENTALISTS ARE FIGHTING science the best they know how—which is not very well—the scientists seem to be turning considerably to religion. At the convention of the American Association for the Advancement of Science, which sat through the turn of the year at Philadelphia, some of the members gave their imaginations unusual scope, as when Director Curtis of Allegheny Observatory, lecturing with a lantern slide that showed the galaxies of stars, contributed the conviction that man's spirit is as immortal as the universe he inhabits. It is not a new thing for astronomers to have pious thoughts. All their studies lead them to that and, indeed, the most religious of all spectacles and the one that most binds the human spirit to the idea of God and the after life is the sight of the sky on a starlit night.

Maybe the newspapers gave disproportionate attention to the more spiritual suggestions of the scientists. They made a great deal, for example, of the paper of Professor Tchijevsky of Moscow, who anticipates great disturbance during the next two years in our terrestrial home as a consequence of intense sun-spot activity. That is not exactly a pious thought but at least it has to do with celestial influences. All great world ructions, this Russian observer said, had followed these periods of sun-spot activity. The periods come in eleven-year cycles: three years of minimum excitability of human beings, two years of increasing excitability, three years of maximum excitability, and then three years of decline to the minimum that closes the cycle. This year and until 1929 the period of sun-spot activity now going on attains its maximum "with resulting human activity of the highest historical importance which may again change the political chart of the world." The more so, he says, because this maximum coincides with the maxima of two other periods of sixty and thirty-five years.

Mr. Tchijevsky's notion is that all human beings are creatures of the sun and its vast electrical power, and that they behave as they do, not for the reasons they imagine, but because the sun influences them. His studies, it seems, have been very extensive, and the mere digest of his theories runs to thirty pages, so that the newspapers gave comparatively little of them; but even that little is interesting. The world does get very crazy at times. Persons not yet killed by motor cars may recall the year 1912 when there was such a curious quiver of behavior and such an extraordinary craze for dancing. That may well have been one of the preliminary periods of the sun-spots cycle which introduced the Great War.

One would like to have some competent person investigate Mr. Tchijevsky's theory, except that anybody considered competent to investigate anything usually does not believe it. It is the incompetent who have belief, though it is true that the competent are improving in that respect. The idea of the influence of the sun on human dispositions and behavior is really not so crazy. It is credible enough that sun spots are a part of the game in which we hold cards, and it is more credible in this decade than it used to be that there is some sense in astrology. Astrology undertakes to determine the influence of heavenly bodies upon human behavior. When one reads that in April Uranus and Saturn "will force changes by making old ways and ideas impossible," it does not sound quite so fantastic as it used to. We are so accustomed nowadays to the notion that the world is changing that we can even look with indulgence upon suggestions about the means by which the changes come to pass. Throughout the year, says a newspaper astrologer, "there will be reverberations of the gathering of the scientists interested in psychics held at Clark University in December, and prevailing materialistic conceptions will be abated. Don't imagine this suggests revolution, because mental changes of any kind move imperceptibly. You simply get up one morning with a different feeling about things to which formerly you were either antagonistic or favorable."

THE idea that force is exerted only by visible and physical means does not go so strong as it used to. We are getting more familiar with the idea of powerful and important forces that are imponderable, invisible, and very imperfectly understood. Rays are going strong in this generation. Sixty years ago people did not count much on rays, but this Russian informant's sun-spot theory—that's rays. Radio is rays. Magnetism is a kind of ray, and nobody seems to know enough about electricity to make it dangerous for anybody else to classify that as a ray. Healing is done increasingly by rays. The spirit doctors work with them—at least so one is told—and no incarnate doctor's shop is fully furnished nowadays without a ray machine of some sort.

Telepathy is almost accepted as a fact, which means that it is accepted by some people whose acceptance is respected. Gilbert Murray, the poet and professor, a particularly honored person whom Harvard University just at this writing has borrowed from Oxford, has himself experimented with it and seems to think well of it. Telepathy is the transfer of ideas from one mind to another without the use of visible, audible or other known physical means. Doctor Murray, as reported in the papers some time ago, seemed persuaded that such a transfer of thought is made. Well if it is, what makes it? What is the process? Something must go from one mind to another. There you get rays again. The mind seems to give out a substance. We have to think in terms of substance. Light is a substance. Thought is a substance. Will is a substance. Spirit is a substance. Our learned brethren doubtless have other names for these things and doubtless better ones. But it does seem to be that these influences give out various kinds of rays made of something; that healing is done in that way; that

the arts of great orators and great actors are connected with an ability to produce rays and shoot
them out.

There is a lot to learn about these matters. We
have got far enough to think that much. What an
orator or an actor may do in producing emotion or
affecting the feelings, a book, a picture, a piece of
music will often do. Maybe books and pictures and
written music are storage batteries. They certainly
hold what is put into them in a fashion truly
remarkable.

Mr. H. G. Wells seems to be of the opinion that
more is going on than usual. He is putting out a
line of newspaper articles about "The Way the
World Is Going" and declares in his announcement
of them that there is a biological revolution in
progress of far profounder moment than any
French or Russian Revolution that ever happened.
He denies the unchangeableness of human life. The
facts, he says:

come dripping in to us, here a paragraph in a newspaper, there
a book, now a chance remark; we are busy about our personal
affairs and rarely find time to sit back and consider the
immense significance of the whole continuing process.

Mr. Wells is not an urgent supporter of the
status quo in this world. No doubt he looks forward cheerfully to fundamental changes. One
would rather trust him though as a forecaster of
change than as an accurate estimator of what will
finally be produced. The urgency of the Russian
gentleman's sun spots will decline in two or three
years; but while they are working, Mr. Wells is

an excellent man to observe their influence on human affairs.

WHOM will the sun spots work for, Smith or Coolidge? That is the political question which may well engage the mind of our politicians. These gentlemen, Governor Smith and President Coolidge, are at present our foremost political figures. Mr. Coolidge stands for prosperity, dividends, and the *status quo*. Governor Smith stands predominantly for revolt. His strength is that he attracts the attention, and so considerably the admiration of people who do not like the way things are going in the United States. If there are to be no changes of great moment Mr. Coolidge is almost an ideal President for us. Everybody whose dividends are satisfactory and whose political thought is first of all for them ought to be pleased with Mr. Coolidge and want to keep him as long as possible. But people who, on the whole, think that current life is not what it ought to be, and want someone as dissimilar from Coolidge as it is safe to follow, are very observant of Alfred Smith and very thoughtful about his powers and qualities. He is far from being a revolutionary character. He is not despondent, not disgruntled, not particularly rebellious, not excessively ambitious. To people who are dissatisfied with our relations to the world outside of the United States he has so far had almost nothing to say.

Mr. Coolidge has confined himself as much as possible to the world within the United States, but as President he has not been able to escape concerns outside of our borders. But Alfred Smith has lived and moved and had his political being not merely within the United States but within the State of New York. As his political reputation all rests upon his public service in that one State, it is the more remarkable how big a reputation it is. It is big because his service to New York has made people familiar with his personality, made them see in him powers that they have admired and qualities that they have trusted. All the same, the reaching out toward him as a candidate of voters who are neither Irish nor Catholic—which of course may not survive for another year—is one expression of a great discontent. To people who do not like the way that life is going here now, or the agents who are directing it, Alfred Smith and his ideas and his behavior are attractive by contrast. When the Protestant churches have done themselves great damage by their squabbles and their blind support of Prohibition, here is Al Smith, a Catholic, and a Wet! He might be both, of course, and have no political strength but, as it is, he exemplifies for many people a better understanding of life, a better practice of living, a much greater ability in public service and a much more Christianized spirit than the more active reformers and drink fighters among the Protestants.

Nothing accounts for him. Not that he is a man of the people, born poor; not that he is a Catholic; not that he is Irish (and one hears he is only half

Irish). Nothing about his religion or his raising
explains him. Evidently he was born so—able, observing, reasoning, conciliating, charming. Somehow he must have had good rays shot into him. A
great talent is Governor Smith, apparently a first-
class actor was lost when he went into politics. If
he runs for President against Mr. Coolidge there
will be a complete contrast of candidates and, pre-
sumably, of backers. It would be very interesting.
It is almost inconceivable that he could win a
presidential election next year, but it would be a
great entertainment to have him try.

NEXT year! Next year! How much will happen before next year? A great deal of trouble
is making of one kind or another. Nicaragua, what
of that? Mexico, what of Mexico?

Saul is again among the Prophets. Mr. Hearst
has come out for the co-operation of the English-
speaking nations in keeping the peace of the world.
Politics does make strange bed fellows. Perhaps it
has dawned on Mr. Hearst that we should be
friendly with at least one family in this world.

Would the nations like us any better if Alfred
Smith were President? They might. He has very
winning ways, that man, and there is no reason why
he should not have a first-class Secretary of State, a
gentleman, to wit, who ran for President last time.
Would he wish to send Cardinal O'Connell as Ambassador to London? He might. He seems to
think well of Cardinals. But probably he would
not, and if he did the Senate would hardly back

him. No great harm, however, if he did, but some
entertainment and enormous indignation.

But with the prospect of such active sun spots it
is extraordinarily difficult to see far ahead. One
can see that Prohibition has got to be overhauled
and greatly improved. One can see how ominously
the Protestant churches have strayed away from
their fundamental obligation to keep liberty alive in
the souls of men. One can see that our relations with
the rest of mankind are not altogether what they
ought to be. One can see that our world is by way of
being stood on its head and that a lot of processes
of improvement are ahead of us which we may not
like. One can see that there is a lot to be done but
not who is going to do it.

Business, they tell us, will be good again hereabouts this year, and yet they gently intimate that
last year was high tide for business, and that prosperity, so much extolled, is passing its peak. Perhaps it won't be unmixed evil to have prosperity sit
down and rest a little. Seasons have their value,
and where it is always summer people get lazy. Besides that, prosperity is expensive to the less prosperous. Prices get adjusted to larger fiscal abilities.
Merchants usually charge what buyers are willing
to pay. When briarwood pipes go to seven dollars
for just a fair one, prosperity seems a bit sarcastic.

How rich it is expedient to be has never been determined either for individuals or for nations.
What is plain enough is that there is a relation between means and duty. Also, that riches are a test
and trial of character. That is just as much true

of nations as it is of men or women. If you have, you must do, on peril of rotting if you don't. If what you ought to do is beyond your ability though not beyond your income that is bad luck. Our country has great power. That is obvious. It seems as yet to be deficient in means to apply that power to the needs of the world. Industrially it does so more or less. Politically it does not. Spiritually it does not seem just at present to be cutting much ice, and yet there is spiritual power enough in the United States if only it can be started. It may be that our great problem this year is the problem of unused powers, and possibly that provision of sun-spot rays, which the Russian scientist predicts, may get us going again. We seem to need something with a kick in it: we really do. Internationally our years of probationary Prohibition have been far from glorious.

Various Loose Ends

HE ADMIRAL WAS SAYING HE NEVER KNEW a man to love a skinny woman, but of course his acquaintance is limited, as anybody's is, and probably he exaggerated. Still, in the main he was plausible, at least. Women, taken by and large, have a propensity not to be skinny and do better to yield to it in moderation rather than to defeat it too much. Apparently, just now they look at the fashion papers and yearn to be thin. Many of them take measures to that effect, and in so doing they flatter one another by showing respect for the opinions of women rather than for those of men.

But from the Admiral, who went on talking, the next echo was that there is no man on earth who cannot be vamped by a woman. Well, yes. Time, place, and person being all favorable, there is probably no man who could not be vamped sometime by some woman, else had Nature planned in vain.

A lady who was listening said she would not give a penny for a man who could not be vamped. Certainly not! (They must have come from reading a murder trial in the papers, a great story of vamping thoroughly done.) A man who could not be vamped would be objectionable, but so

would a man too easily vamped. There is that
story of Joseph, held up to admiration or the
contrary these many centuries as the unvampable
hero. Nonsense! It does not follow that because
Joseph escaped Mrs. Potiphar that he could not be
vamped. In that particular case his whole integrity as a trustworthy person was involved, and
he had sense enough to know that there was nothing for him but to run for it. That he was falsely
accused and sent to jail was a bagatelle compared
with the other situation into which he would have
fallen in his master's house if he had not escaped.
A great injustice is done to Joseph by supposing
he could not be vamped. He was a remarkable
man; as remarkable as any ever Plutarch told of;
but he was not a monster.

Talk ran on to government. Someone quoted
Kerensky as saying that Russia is no democracy.
Opinion was offered by the Admiral that Italy is
the only democracy to-day and is the only place
where labor unions really have a voice. As for us
in the United States, he thought we lived nowadays
in an industrial monarchy; certainly not in a democracy. But does that mean more than that,
having grown enormously and come to mass production in most other things, we work it naturally
and inevitably in politics, and instead of leading
our brother by the hand to the polls, we get him
there by organization and advertisement and even
cut a melon for him if necessary? Just now,
between elections, our government may seem to be
an industrial monarchy or oligarchy; but wait a

little. Henry Ford's idea that the higher the wages the greater the buying power and the better for business is a good idea while it lasts but, like most other ideas, it is probably subject to jolts. People who have something definite and marketable to sell may see their advantage in a very liberal provision of possible buyers with funds. People who are sledding along and trying to make a living and live on it are liable to be embarrassed when called upon to pay a mechanic a dollar and a half, or more, an hour. In due time it would seem that there will be quite an earnest reconsideration of the purchasing power of money and a new diffusion of the idea once so prevalent that every man should be his own mechanic.

So proceeded the diagnosis of the political situation and went on to things spiritual and how to save the world. What was salvation and what was the means of it? A lady contributed that "somehow what is true about Blackmanism ought to be said; what is true of his work and its results —not to answer lies but to show what is going on."

"Blackman! Blackman! Well, what about him?"

The Admiral and the Lawyer perked up a little. "Who is Blackman?"

"Oh, don't you know about Blackman? Blackman* is a changer of men. Harold Begbie wrote a book about him, now republished here."

"Well, now, who is Harold Begbie?"

* F. N. D. Buchman.

"Bless me. How ignorant you are! Begbie is the Englishman who wrote the *Mirrors of Downing Street* and who years before, along about 1910, put out a very remarkable book, *Twice Born Men*, about the spiritual exploits of the Salvation Army and how men were changed by it. Of that book we are told that William James said his *Varieties of Religious Experience* might be called a postscript to it. Begbie disclosed how a work of grace was done in very hard characters by the Salvation Army, and how these characters, born again, went around in the same bodies as before, but transmogrified as to their spiritual insides. The bodies had belonged to bad characters and looked it. After the resident characters had changed, the bodies continued to look as before, though their occupants no longer behaved to match them. It takes time, of course, for a transformed spirit to modify the aspects of the body that it dwells in."

So Begbie having written that remarkable book about the Salvation Army, and being considerably addicted to religion and its power to change men, when Blackman turned up with symptoms of remarkable faculties as a changer, took notice of Blackman, and in due time wrote him up in a book published here under the title of *More Twice Born Men*. As lately reprinted in this country its name is *Life Changers*. Blackman is an American, has traveled everywhere, lived around generally from China to Peru, and changed men and women, more or less, wherever he has lived, and has been the subject of extensive, controversial discussion

running at times to acrimony, as especially disclosed not long since in Princeton, New Jersey.
The demand for religion is steady and even clam-
orous just now, and anybody that can put it over is
interesting. We have thousands of earnest workers
who can organize, operate typewriters, appeal for
funds, get them, spend them. Of what can be accomplished by means of that sort we have mass
production in a measure that is highly gratifying
to some people and rather appalling to others, but
of the ability to put over religion there is no surfeit.
The demand exceeds the supply. In so far as
Blackman can do it, Blackman is an interesting
fellow.

The lady on the southeast corner of the table
had seen him do it. She said, "He makes the
Holy Spirit as practical as a telephone with a
voice on the other end. Blackman does not wait
for this power to drop into people's laps; he teaches
them how to get it. I never had any feeling of
being able to hook onto religion. My sister, who
had it, couldn't make me even understand what it
was about. Nobody thought it worth while to try.
But Blackman did. The Blackmanites are dead
sure that each of us is due for a personal acquaint-
anceship with God, and they have the experience
and the technique, and help you get it."

Blackman has the use of a house in New York
at which the people he deals with meet and discuss
religion and their experiences of it. There, too,
a smaller circle of people who work with him have
what they call house parties. They dine together,

each one paying the cost of his entertainment. The house is the headquarters of Blackman's proceedings in New York. He does not live there, but his office is there. "He is a man," said the informing lady, "who spends nothing on himself. The funds that support his movement are furnished to him by people who are interested. A few give generously, many give a very little, but he sails as close to the wind as an apostle and often checks out all he has to help somebody."

THESE doings, it seems, do not proceed without searching criticism. People who do not understand about the possibilities of spiritual changes in other people with resulting improvement in their characters and deportment look for ulterior motives in Blackman's activities. There are various theories about him, and he seems to be pretty carefully watched by persons who want to know. Since he is not infallible, it is quite possible that some of his methods are reasonably criticized, and that the results of the exercise of his interesting powers are not always immediately fortunate. But Blackman goes on his way with very little noise and no attempt to secure ordinary advertisement. Unlike Aimee McPherson, he never deals with large audiences. His faculty is not that of the exhorter of crowds. He deals best with individuals or with small companies where the talk is quite familiar.

What is this change he brings about in some people and how does he do it? What power does he use? To answer that would carry one, no doubt, into psychology. Probably William James has discussed it, and people who read the New Testament may get light about it from that source. To Begbie, who writes about him, some ideas and processes to which Blackman imputes great value, seem unimportant. Begbie is greatly impressed with the value of what Blackman does, but not sure that Blackman understands how he does it. It is something like Al Smith and the encyclicals. He does not feel that they are important to religion as he knows it, and says they are not binding on him, and has clerical support in that opinion. That is one of the important details in his letter. Truth is, that what is important in the Christian religion as stated and defined for us at this time, and what is unimportant or obsolete, is one of the big questions of the day. It is at the root of the rows between the Modernists and the Fundamentalists and between the Protestants and the Roman Catholics. Almost everyone will agree that there is a liberal infusion of the Christian religion in the Roman Catholic Church. Most people will agree that there is a lot of it in the Protestant churches; that the Quakers have it; that thousands have it and work it who are not connected with a church organization, but when it comes to details of statement about what is necessary to salvation and what is immaterial, they are apt to go up in the air.

Probably as knowledge increases and study con-

tinues there will be better understanding of these
difficult matters, and as the essentials become apparent and the unessentials fade out there may
be a better agreement between sects. There is
better agreement now than there used to be; very
much better. When it is said that there must be
a restatement of religious truth the answer is apt
to be—"Not yet. We have not quite come to it."
That may be a wise answer, for new definitions
will not help until the substance of them has
already been reached by most of the people concerned.

One thing that is coming in nowadays for re-
vision is the old idea of God as a powerful and
rather irritable magnate, for whom it is expedient
to watch out. More and more people come to
realize that when it comes to defining the Almighty
they haven't the qualifications to do it. In spite
of the mechanistic theory of the universe and everything of that sort, the belief in God seems to go
as strong as ever in the world nowadays, though
the understanding of Him halts, observing and
speculating, and waits, not without reverence, for
more light. There is an order in the universe;
there are laws of life, spiritual, mental, physical.
When we disturb the order or violate the laws
"God is offended" as heretofore, and we suffer.
But we don't express it so nowadays. Neither do
we attempt pacification by burnt offerings. Nevertheless, the fundamentals haven't changed much.
It is merely that we express them differently.

Begbie thinks theological seminaries are awful places for young men. He thinks that theological students should be learning about life and how to help it rather than about theologies. Perhaps some of our American seminaries do better than he knows. The best of them undoubtedly try to keep up to the date.

"They do indeed," said the lady in the southeast corner. "I know one where some of the students are studying spiritism and not illicitly either, but at the instigation of their boss. At last accounts that reached me they had 'levitation' of objects and an intelligent 'control,' and the apparent beginning of an 'independent voice.' Think of that in a theological seminary! You can't say of all of them they are not willing to learn."

Doubtless Begbie would agree with Young Publius that the way to study religion is by the case system. That is precisely the way he has studied Blackman. It is Blackman's facts that make him interesting, not his theories about them. A lot of people in this world need to be changed: radically changed in their understanding of life, their aspirations, and their deportment. If there is to be peace in the world the job of changing them must go forward on a large scale. Anyone who works at it successfully, even in a limited degree, is interesting. Of course it is the job of the Churches, and they do more at it than they get credit for just now; but there is a great company of people whom they do not reach and will not reach until something happens which will greatly increase their efficiency. But still the job goes forward in all kinds of ways, many of them highly obnoxious to orthodox persons. Christian Scientists seem to make better lives. Whatever the merits or the defects of their theories, in their practice they change people, and so do other more or less organized activities of that sort. They change people and help them to live. No doubt the Unity Society of Kansas City does it. The Spiritists do it in a way, at least some of them do. It is not altogether extravagant even to say that there is something spiritual about Spiritualism, but there really is if you get hold of it. Studying religion by the case system one would run down these different activities or as many as he could, and try to discover what made them go,—what the battery was. In all of them that are any good the battery, the source of energy, is probably the same, and if you can draw on that, however you do it, you are likely to get results.

Re-Discovering Europe

T WAS A REAL FAIRY STORY, THAT STORY of Lindbergh—something between the Arabian Nights and Hans Andersen or Laboulaye: Prince Charming dropping out of the sky and allaying all the rows and making everybody happy. Even two months afterwards it may not be too late to talk about it, for really it is an astonishing subject.

The miracle of Lindbergh was not so much in his getting across to Paris as in the extraordinary effect that his exploit seemed to have had on the human race. The human race—hardly less—for when the newspapers and the radios and all the picture-taking machines and the movies and the loud speakers got through with Lindbergh's exploit, the bigger part of mankind must surely have heard of it. Here was a most individual feat, something done by that youth primarily out of his own head, with only so much consultation with others as was necessary to convert them to the idea that his thought was feasible and offered a good chance for success. Charles did the stunt himself but, of course, he had organization back of him and under him at every turn. It made his engine, it made his plane, it made the noise he started with, and amplified and distributed the resounding acclamation of his landing on Bourget Field.

There are at least two kinds of renown. That which proceeds from a great life, or an episode in a great life, and that which comes from a great stunt. St. Paul, for example, is a very renowned person. His reputation grew out of the years of his ministry and especially from the deep impression made by his writings. But there was Leonidas, another deathless name, but his renown all due to one great exploit in which the leader and his companions finally perished. Leonidas certainly shot his bolt. So did St. Paul. One took half a week and the other, I suppose, half a lifetime. Yet the glory of Leonidas, and that of Lindbergh too, was more than mere stunt-fame. For both it was the fruit of long training and of reasoned and resolute purpose in minds that saw a task and accepted it, risks and all. And in both cases the end justified the risk.

Renown seems to depend upon the telling. Whoever told of Leonidas—Herodotus, Thucydides— whoever it was—did a thorough job. St. Paul in the main was his own biographer and good at it, certainly. But for Lindbergh there worked instantly and then for days together the whole apparatus of publicity of our contemporary world. Nine-day wonders are not common. Already at this writing Lindbergh has held the front-page headlines far longer than that. He has a monopoly of spotlight publicity ahead of him and wonders at it. My, my, how much is in the telling!

Perhaps Dædalus did fly, but was inadequately reported. It is easier to believe in the knowledge and the exploits of our predecessors on this earth than it used to be. Think of the pre-Columbian discoverers of America! A new one is uncovered every now and then. Apparently there were Europeans as well as Asiatics here long before Columbus. That is as good as known, but it was not known at the time. There was no machinery for getting the news about Norsemen, Icelanders, Greenlanders, fishermen who got to Brazil and other fishermen who caught cod on Newfoundland Banks, and got ashore. Whoever heard their stories? They say Columbus did read somebody's story. Nevertheless, it seems that things not known about avail not much more than things not done at all; and somewhere in this is to be found one of the great superiorities of our age to any other that we know of. It is the most published age that ever was. This is not all to the advantage of happiness, but it may considerably be to the profit of knowledge. The machine on which Charles Lindbergh rode to Paris was a good machine, it is true; but really it was nothing to the machine in which inevitably and unexpectedly he found himself embarked when he got there. Quite beyond his expectation, he sped aboard our current world's enormous mechanism of publicity and aboard it at this writing he still remains.

It is getting easier than it was to believe in inspiration; in our guidance by guardian angels and spiritual beings concerned to keep us on the right

track if possible. Charles' behavior in the car of
publicity favors the idea that he has a competent
guardian angel who is very steady on the job.
Never anybody behaved any better under upsetting
circumstances nor bore being heroized with better
humor or more disarming grace. We all say that
he behaved "so naturally," and in so saying we pay
a compliment to ourselves and to mankind in
general. If to behave as simply as Charles did is
natural, why, we must all be nice people in the
making even though we may not all be developed
yet. Think of all the elaborate efforts that have been
made to bring the inhabitants of earth, or at least
what we call the Western nations, into agreement.
Think of all the conferences, negotiations, exhorta-
tions, treaties and entreaties all aimed to bring a
better spirit in the world and get the nations out
of the habit of snarling at one another. Then
think of the opinion of the United States that has
prevailed in Western Europe for many months past
with Uncle Sam in the rôle of Uncle Shylock,
and all that. Then lo, over night comes Prince
Charming in his car, and a vast roar rises from
the Danube to the Atlantic—"This is a lovely man,
so brave, so modest, so skillful, so unconcerned for
money! Surely, after all, the Americans must be
quite good people. *Vive* the United States!"

It reminds one of what William James said
about the possible value of spiritualism to revive
faith in Christianity, a revival which could hardly
come, he thought, without a belief in new physical

facts and possibilities, such as had attended the origin of all religions. "A glimpse," he said, "into a world of new phenomenal possibilities enveloping those of the present life would do in an instant what abstract considerations about the reality of the moral order would not do in a year." Some such glimpse as that Europe seems to have had when Lindbergh dropped down on Bourget Field.

Now then, what may we hope that Charles will accomplish which will be worth all this immense noise made about him and which we do not wish to see go to waste?

He has taken us out from under the spell of the movie idols and the fisticuff champions, and lighted up our minds by contemplation of an achievement of a higher order. A newspaper writer, Mr. Garrett, has said (in the *World*) that he has lifted up men's respect for mankind as it has not been done since his predecessors died in war.

So he has, and it is a very great achievement and most timely.

In doing so he has acquired immense influence. How will he use that?

So far as one can judge, he will use it to quicken the development of aviation in these States.

And that may be immensely important, not primarily for commercial reasons, but to increase our efficiency in war, and so our influence and power as a factor in keeping the peace of the world

and saying our say in international concerns at
a time when great changes are making, and still
greater ones impending.

My very accomplished friend Weston was talking the other day about the immediate future of the
world and of wars to come, and doped it out something like this. "What I go by," he said, "is this:
A nation that is ashamed of itself recovers its self-
respect *through war*. The French had disgraced
themselves by the Revolution and were very grateful to Napoleon for giving them *glory*. The
Germans never got over the humiliation that they
had been subjected to through war. The Italians
have never quite got over the humiliation of their
centuries of division under Austria. They have
had the inferiority complex. Mussolini relies on
that. Russia for the same reason will follow."
So he figured out that "Italy will make war in
1934 and Russia in 1950."

All that is interesting in a way. The year 1934
is only seven years ahead of us and some people
now living may survive till 1950. But Lindbergh's
hop and its astonishing emotional consequences, followed and intensified by the exploit of Chamberlin
and Levine, is fit to remind betters that it is the
unexpected that usually happens. Weston's forecasts seem to be based on conditions of life that
existed before the Great War. There are now
tremendous motives for the maintenance of peace
and terrific objections to large-scale war of which
humanity was certainly not so conscious before

1914. One can understand how an inferiority complex turns to glory. One can also understand that it was a comfort to many minds who were tired of having debt collection the chief subject of discussion between their country and Europe to see that subject suddenly swept out of notice by the appearance in Paris of a young man in an airplane. As between Weston's calculations and those of the British-Israel people who start calamities in May of next year and carry them along till 1936, anyone can have his choice, or reject both if he prefers.

All the same, while interest in aviation in general has been wonderfully increased by these daring ventures of Lindbergh and Chamberlin, and while the commercial possibilities of air service to Europe are now actively discussed, a very lively detail— perhaps the predominant one—of the talk about these hopes is their relation to war—the next war, the thought of which no one is willing to countenance, but which few reflecting people can yet dismiss from their minds. The flights have made the world smaller. Commander Byrd with a bigger airplane and several engines in it has carried that effect still farther. It is a small world when you can go from New York to Paris on one load of gasoline in a day and a half, and these machines steadily progressing in efficiency and safety can be turned into missile-carriers if occasion calls for it. They can drop their bad bombs on far-off places. It has all made the people whose minds are on war think harder than ever on that subject.

BUT it has seemed to help to tie together Western Europe and the United States, and that is very valuable, even though the tie made seems no more than sentimental; for a sentimental tie may be very strong—indeed, the strongest kind.

When we think about war, another Great War, of course we think about Germany and whether she will tie up with Russia to beat France and Britain, or tie up with Western Europe to stand off Muscovy and anything that might threaten in Asia. If there is a magic of conciliation in these visits of airmen it was a particularly good thing to have Chamberlin and Levine land in Germany at the home of Luther, and make their first popular appearance in Berlin. Perhaps that will do good; and anything that promotes good-will between Germany and the nations whom she lately fought is very valuable indeed, and all the more so since the Soviet agents and representatives have been thrown out of London.

Mussolini's Italy is a political conundrum. Which way will that cat jump? Turkey is another. But the big one is Russia. There are very active minds in that great country nowadays and they seem to practice day and night for the realization of purposes that run constantly through them to produce extremely radical changes in this world. The changes they are concerned about are not the evolutionary ones that are going on everywhere, but changes, apparently, that are geared to a plan; a tremendous plan to make Russia offhand the dominant political and economic influence in human life. If that plan ever runs strong enough to be recognized as an imminent world peril, what is the United States going to do about it? It has refused diplomatic relations with Russia. It has done that much already. Britain, who needed them and somewhat reluctantly accepted them, has had to give them up. That was evidenced as far as it went of like-mindedness between the British government and ours. What should we do if we saw another irrepressible conflict, not merely between nations of Western Europe, but between Western Europe and those minds that plan at Moscow, and all the backing they could gather? It is not necessary to say what the United States would do; but as one thinks about it, these airplane exploits take on a new significance that is quite comforting. For if there is another big disturbance in the world, the armies of the sky are going to count enormously, and the influence of the United States may be vitally increased by the reputation of its airmen and the provision of means on a large scale to make their proficiency effective.

Our country has seemed somewhat torpid since the Armistice about saving the world, albeit it has done far better than the world as a rule has given it credit for, for it has provided money, and it has furnished service at times which has been extremely valuable. But Lindbergh and Chamberlin will be taken as evidence that it is waking up. They have carried us back to Europe in an astonishing degree, in a fashion and to an extent that is altogether outside of calculation or foresight. It is almost as if they had discovered a new world, and in so far as it is that, the discovery is very, very timely. For how very unreal our present world is, particularly to the elders in it! The young who never knew a different one, probably do not feel this unreality, but the changes that have come in the twentieth century have been enormous, and minds that go back of them and to nineteenth-century habits and standards seem to themselves to be living in a sort of dreamland—much of it quite delectable, but a lot of it pretty well passing understanding. Does anyone, do you suppose, look upon our present world, our present life, with any sense of its permanency? Is everybody waiting for something to drop, or only meditating elders and international politicians? Most curious times, times apparently of preparation and subject evidently to unexpected thrills.

INDEX